# Preaching with All You've Got

*For*

*John Pritchard, Dale Hanson,*
*Geoffrey Stevenson and Walter Moberly*

*Partners in the gospel*
*and, in the style of Barnabas,*
*Sons of encouragement*

# Preaching with All You've Got

# Embodying the Word

## David Day

HENDRICKSON
PUBLISHERS

PREACHING WITH ALL YOU'VE GOT: EMBODYING THE WORD
Hendrickson Publishers, Inc.
P. O. Box 3473
Peabody, Massachusetts 01961-3473

ISBN 1-59856-029-8

Originally published under the title *Embodying the Word*
First published in Great Britain in 2005
Society for Promoting Christian Knowledge
36 Causton Street
London SW1P 4ST
Copyright © David Day 2005

*First Printing Hendrickson Publishers' edition — April 2006*

*Printed in the United States of America*

**Library of Congress Cataloging-in-Publication Data**

Day, David, 1936–
    [Embodying the Word]
    Preaching with all you've got : embodying the Word / David Day.
        p. cm.
    Originally published: Embodying the Word. London : Society for Promoting Christian Knowledge, c2005.
    Includes bibliographical references (p. ).
    ISBN 1-59856-029-8 (alk. paper)
    1. Preaching. I. Title.
    BV4211.3.D39 2006
    251—dc22
                                        2006043396

# Contents

# 1 Putting flesh on the bones

*The embodied Word*

We all know John Bunyan's *Pilgrim's Progress* but his *Seasonable Counsel* is less familiar. In this book Bunyan is reflecting on the fact that, more often than not, disaster strikes without warning. To illustrate his point he turns to the account of John the Baptist's execution (Mark 6.17–29), but tells the story in a startling and original way:

> 'And immediately the King sent an executioner and commanded his head to be brought' (Mark 6.27). The story is concerning Herod and John the Baptist. Herod's dancing girl had begged John Baptist's head, and nothing but his head must serve her turn.
>
> 'Well, girl, thou shalt have it.'
>
> 'Have it? Aye, but it will be long first.'
>
> 'No, thou shalt have it now! Just now! Immediately!'
>
> And immediately he sent an executioner and commanded his head to be brought.
>
> Here is sudden work for sufferers. Here is no intimation beforehand.
>
> The executioner comes to John – now! Whether he was at dinner or asleep or whatever he was about. The bloody man bolts in upon him and the first word he salutes him with is:
>
> 'Sir, strip! Lay down your neck! For I come to take away your head.'
>
> 'But hold! Stay! Wherefore? Pray, let me commit my soul to God.'
>
> 'No, I must not stay. I am in haste!'
>
> Slap says his sword. And off falls the good man's head.
>
> This is sudden work, work that stays for no man.[1]

Do we preach like that? Even as you read the words you are taken into the scene. When you speak them aloud, you are almost compelled to act them out. Bunyan doesn't insert phrases such as: 'he said', 'she retorted', but chooses to carry the narrative forward by direct speech. I imagine that his hands and his face were involved as well. Can you say 'Slap!' without some kind of gesture? Even the accompanying commentary is pared down in order that the listener can be plunged back into the action. Such preaching is vivid and engaging. What Bunyan has done is *embody the message.*

## A WORD IN FLESH

Bunyan's method is an example of the central theme of this book: *in what different ways can preachers embody the Word?* Even a moment's thought suggests that they use a variety of methods. Most obviously, they flesh out their messages in the words they choose, but we should not forget that the personality of the preacher is also a powerful medium of communication. Sometimes they embody ideas by interacting with objects and pictures; sometimes they achieve this aim by engaging with literature and drama. And all preachers hope that, when the sermon has done its work, the message will be embodied in the responses of the congregation. The theme is clearly one of immense importance, especially in the light of the rather sad comment, 'The Word became flesh and is become word again.' I think it was Aquinas who said: 'Nothing is present in the intellect that was not previously present in the senses.' Is it possible to make the return journey?

This approach is a homiletical version of the principle of incarnation. The spiritual can be found in the material and needs the material to make itself fully known. There have always been traditions within Christianity which have been suspicious of the sacramental, elevating word and thought above action or symbol. And there have certainly been traditions of preaching which have prized information over image, doctrine over story, the intellect over the emotions and the soul over the flesh.

Many writers have commented on how this tension plays out. For example, the Roman Catholic preacher Walter Burghardt focuses on the way *words* are used in sermons: 'Although God's grace is all-powerful, it dashes against two obstacles: a homilist dead below the larynx, and a minimal vocabulary dominated by abstract nouns ending in -tion.'[2]

In the same style, Stephen Fowl and Gregory Jones have questioned traditions which exaggerate the image of *preacher* as herald. They query a model of preaching which sometimes seems to separate Word and person, and rail against 'That faceless reading and witness in which it is presumed that the messenger is irrelevant to the message.'[3]

How might this move towards embodiment show up in practice? It will mean a preference for the concrete over against the abstract, for the specific over the general, for images rather than precepts, for stories rather than distillations of truth, for instances and examples rather than general statements. It will prize a word made flesh, whether that is the Word refracted through the unique personality of this particular preacher or embodied in a specific cultural artefact.

All these examples are aspects of the old maxim, 'Show rather than tell.' This doesn't mean, of course, that we never have a use for the abstract, the concept, the doctrinal formulation, the precept or the general principle. But 'Show rather than tell' nudges us towards finding ways of making an idea live, breathe and dance in front of our congregation's eyes. A word is not just an entry in the dictionary: it is coloured by living experience. Calvin Miller draws our attention to the model of Jesus: 'Remember the Word is more than word; the Word has been made flesh!'[4]

## WHAT KIND OF A BOOK?

If embodying the Word is the theme, then what kind of book is this? My intention is that it should be primarily a practical workbook. Books on the theory and theology of preaching abound, and something of a homiletics industry has grown up in the USA.[5] While I have profited enormously from the experts, I have not tried to emulate them here, even if I were capable of doing so. My major interest is in the craft of preaching, and this book is designed to be of use in preparing next Sunday's sermon. Since it is a workbook you will find two or three exercises included in each chapter. I have to confess that I sometimes skip these when I read workbooks but, since they are intended to be useful, I hope that you are more conscientious than I am.

Books which have an axe to grind risk being rigidly doctrinaire. The reader soon forms the impression that there is only one way to do it. I was told as a boy playing tennis never, ever, to use two hands on the backhand. Then I saw Pancho Segura play at Wimbledon and, yes, he employed a double-handed backhand. Since then a stream of professional players have discovered that the sky does not fall down if you use two hands.

A more important consideration than 'This is the way to do it' is 'Will other ways work as well?' If you suspect that dogma is taking over from commonsense, put the book down and go and have a cup of tea. Nevertheless I do believe that my general approach is worth giving a try.

In a book about embodying ideas, one example must be better than ten precepts. For that reason I have included lots of excerpts from real sermons. It will help if you read them aloud or at least hear them in your head. Scanning them as a literary piece will mean that they lose their oral quality, and all of them were written to be spoken. Examples not only make a principle concrete and show what it might look like in practice, they also encourage everyone to have a go for themselves. I am sure that there are dozens of different ways of preaching a sermon, so let's experiment, share our findings and vary our standard way of preaching. I am very grateful to all who have allowed me to use their material. Sometimes we hug our sermons to us with the attitude, 'Don't you touch my baby.' It's refreshing to acknowledge the generosity of all those who have let me push the pram for a while.

By the end you will probably have worked out that I am male, white, Anglican, ordained and living in the north east of England. Despite these disadvantages I hope the book will be relevant to all who preach, whether male or female, old or young, Anglican, Roman Catholic, Free Church, lay or ordained, Jew or Greek, bond or free. Most of the material has been trialled at cross-denominational conferences, diocesan and circuit groups, with readers, clergy and local preachers, in colleges and courses. At times I may seem to imply that what is normal for me should be normative for everyone else. I ask you to believe that it's unintentional.

## THE SCOPE OF THE BOOK

How is the Word embodied? I guess most of us will turn first to the person of the preacher, and Part 1 examines this theme. A sermon involves a human being standing up and claiming in some sense to speak for God. Like it or not, we cannot avoid embodying the message. Naturally, we would all like to feel that we were transparent to God and that something of his nature was communicated through us. Moses' face shone, the apostles were recognized as 'having been with Jesus', Paul knew that the treasure of the gospel lived in him, even though he was an earthen vessel.

4

Embodying the Word is not just a matter of using words in a particular way: it goes to the heart of who we are.

Now precisely because the whole self is involved we are confronted with a range of issues: theological and practical questions about the preacher's spiritual life, the peculiar temptations which afflict God's representative in the pulpit, the use of personal disclosure in sermons, the place of vulnerability and woundedness, making 'a visceral connection with scripture' and the embodiment of the Word in delivery and 'pulpit performance'.

Part 2 looks more closely at the crafting of words and illustrates the movement from precept, proposition, principle, doctrine, truth, general statement and abstraction towards the specific and the concrete, to sermons that embody a message in imaginative elaborations of a Bible passage, in analogies and metaphors, in instances, examples, stories, dilemmas and illustrations.

Part 3 suggests ways in which preachers can work with the Word when it is embodied in what can be seen or touched. In many sermons the words that are spoken interact with the visual arts (pictures, photos, icons) or find a focus in religious artefacts or everyday objects. Furthermore, when our culture wishes to communicate the myths by which people make sense of their lives, it naturally turns to narrative. People in situations, expressing hopes, fears, values and a vision of the world by living through stories are the heart of TV drama, novels and films. Preachers cannot ignore this rich source of material ready to hand but may still need guidance on how to use it for the best. Finally, in our present context, it is essential to explore the possibilities of computer presentation programs such as PowerPoint, whether tool or master, trying to identify what they do well and where they can work against the grain of preaching.

Sermons take on a life of their own once they have been preached. Preachers hope that their words will be embodied in the lived experience of the congregation, that they will preach, in James Nieman's words, 'sermons that drive people from the church – to live out the message in the world'. Part 4 asks how preaching can encourage active response, both within the time of the sermon and in the rest of the service. Should preachers have an idea of what they want their sermons to do? Is the idea of 'behavioural purpose' unspiritual or manipulative? What different responses are possible? And how is the Word to be expressed in the world once the congregation has left the church?

Calvin Miller tells an engaging story about an anatomy course he took while at college. There was a skeleton in the lecture room which the students nicknamed Caroline. There was also a student named Bonnie in the class. Miller observes that Caroline and Bonnie were structurally similar but adds: 'But I dated Bonnie.'[6] Of course he did! Bonnie was flesh and blood. This book is about turning Carolines into Bonnies.

## THE NOBLE ARMY OF MARTYRS

This is the proper point at which to thank those who have helped me bring the book into the light. First, I am grateful to all the groups who have worked on the material in preaching workshops. In many cases they were unknowing guinea pigs but their comments and reactions gave me valuable feedback and sometimes their body language supplied me with more information than I needed. Then there are those friends and colleagues who were not agile or devious enough to escape being dragooned into reading chapters. Because they were on my side they told me what they thought, sometimes robustly but always courteously. So thank you to Peter Johnson, Tim Sanderson, Walter Moberly, Dale Hanson, Kate Byrom, Judith Ashurst, Geoffrey Stevenson, Kate Macpherson, Andrew Trigger, Gavin and Fran Wakefield, Colin and Rosie Patterson, Ann and Peter West, and John Pritchard. Jamie Byrom, Colin Jones, Jean Tyers, Jill Drury and Tim Sanderson commented specifically on PowerPoint.

No words can do justice to the help and support I have received from my wife, Rosemary. She alone knows the full story but she will not thank me for going into detail in public.

Finally, I want to express my gratitude to four friends who have been companions in the preaching task for many years. Between them they have modelled responsible reading of scripture, imaginative preaching, lively engagement with contemporary culture and faithful friendship. So many lunches and suppers (and breakfasts) and so much laughter. So thank you, John Pritchard, Dale Hanson, Geoffrey Stevenson and Walter Moberly. It is a pleasure to dedicate this book to you in affectionate friendship.

# PART 1

*The Word embodied in the preacher*

# 2  To be a window through thy grace

## *The transparency of the preacher*

'To be a window through thy grace.' The line from George Herbert high-lights something strange, wonderful and inconvenient about preaching. The poet is sure that the preacher is 'a brittle, crazy glass' but sees that, under God, 'doctrine and life, colours and light' can so combine that the human being can become a window for God's life to shine through.[1] That's the vision; it's also the awkward bit.

In the world outside the church there are many situations where everyone accepts that you can give out messages without being personally committed to them. My postman delivers mail whether he approves of it or not; an employee manages to speak on behalf of the firm without her whole life being involved. No doubt it would be helpful not to say too loudly that you think this free offer is a scam or that the managing director is totally corrupt, but it is still possible to dissociate yourself from the message.

It is much more difficult for preachers to stand aside from the words they speak. Preaching is intrinsically self-involving. Behind every sermon lie some disturbing assumptions: that the words you utter have in some way been given you by God; that your life is shaped by the scriptures you expound; that the people you address are brothers and sisters – not cus-tomers, clients or victims. In addition, the sermon connects with activities which cannot be detached from who you are. Worship, prayer, a declara-tion of faith, a call to repentance or rededication involve your inner life. You cannot comfortably just go through the motions.

The preacher is expected to embody the message. It's not merely a matter of using words in a persuasive way. The congregation assumes that we mean what we say and seldom asks us, 'Do you actually believe that stuff or are you just paid to say it?' It isn't only the congregation's view either. We ourselves feel that what we are ought to match what we proclaim and are uneasy when it doesn't. Standing in the pulpit takes us directly into questions of personal integrity, authenticity, holiness and transparency. We want to be WYSIWYG preachers where what the congregation sees is what it gets. Kierkegaard said of John Chrysostom: 'He gesticulated with his whole existence.'[2] I imagine that most of us like the sound of that. We want to be like the rock we buy at the seaside, carrying the same message right through from one end to the other.

As we know, it isn't always like that. There are some dramatic examples of sensational failures to live what you preach. Televangelists caught out in extra-marital affairs repent on screen and at length. A minister is arrested for a nasty piece of fraud and the community is deeply damaged when the truth comes out: 'All the time he was working through that series on Psalm 23 he had his hand in the till and was hard at it embezzling the funds.' Even in the nineteenth century, Spurgeon told his students: 'We have all heard the story of the man who preached so well and lived so badly, that when he was in the pulpit everybody said he should never come out again, and when he was out of it, they all declared he never ought to enter it again.'[3] It would all be much simpler if there was no obligation to match one's life to one's message, but God has not given us that option.

## A BRITTLE, CRAZY GLASS

How does integrity get damaged? There are a number of danger signals.

1   *When the lived life is at odds with the words in the pulpit.* It's easy to go straight to the dramatic examples. They are the stuff of headlines: 'Minister runs off with organist's wife', 'Caught in the web: vicar surfs the Net for naughty photos', and so on. But much more common are less dramatic examples about personal practice and spirituality. If the preacher is vain and openly critical of others, or shows no concern for them, then the words are bound to sound hollow. If I am motivated more by the fact that I have to preach than by the love of God then I am likely to sound like an empty cymbal. Spurgeon called such people 'clockwork ministers'. He said that they were 'not alive by abiding grace within, but are wound up by temporary influences'.[4]

2   *When the words lose contact with reality.* The constant temptation when preaching is not to tell it like it is. Purple passages sound good in the pulpit but the actual life of faith is often a more mundane business. Sermons force you to sound the organ note. Like the liturgy, they

move language into overdrive. We are required to say profound and world-shattering, life-changing things twice a week. Under the pressure we learn how to live with radical claims and demanding values. An air of unreality clings to the great affirmations. We lose the prose – that is, the sense that much of the time the Christian life is ordinary, routine, bread and butter, get-on-with-it, muddle along. It's easy to slip into Mother's Day language ('You are the best mother in all the world') or the funeral eulogy ('George never uttered a cross word, never had an uncharitable thought'). After a while we learn not to be entirely honest.

Now, of course preaching has to deal in poetry and offer an alternative vision to the taken-for-granted world. But too many high-flown phrases make you deaf. Somewhere inside, if you're lucky, a voice of realism says: 'Is that really the way it is? Come off it. You've made it too beautiful, too easy, too victorious. Too many promises, too much poetry.' I remember a young Christian agonizing about the life of discipleship. 'Why does it have to be so hard?' she asked. An older Christian said: 'It will get easier, when you have learned more Bible verses and are able to use them as Jesus did'. Mmm. Perhaps. If only holiness came so smoothly. We need to stay in touch with reality or our listeners will sense that life and sermon inhabit parallel universes.

3 *When the product is not the result of prayer, meditation and seeking the face of God.* Every preacher knows the pressure to skip the bit about waiting on God. It's Wednesday, and Sunday morning's coming. Get to the commentaries as quickly as possible and never mind prayer. Better still, go to a decent website (Sermon Central will do) and draw from their vast database of 60,000 sermons. But whatever you do, get something down on paper.

The temptation to cut corners is beautifully captured by James Nieman:

As the pressures of parish life mount and as the 'urgent' supplants what is genuinely important, we say, 'Well, it won't hurt if just this week I don't spend quite as much time on sermon preparation.' And lo and behold, we are absolutely right! They love us anyway! 'Good sermon,' they continue to chime at the door. Week by week we learn to get by with less and less text study, prayer and reflection. And everything works out fine so long as we just use lots of inflection, including touching illustrations, reinforce the dominant values, and wink, 'Isn't that right, Agnes?' to the congregational president. 'Just such is our case,' said Chrysostom sixteen centuries ago, 'when we make it our aim to be admired, not to instruct; to delight, not prick to the heart; to be applauded and depart with praise, not to correct human manners.'[5]

4    *When we are at ease in the Holy of Holies.* After a while we can begin to forget that we handle holy things. The long-standing suspicion of craft in the sermon and of rhetoric as manipulation is not completely unjustified. I remember a Pentecostal minister admitting that he knew exactly how to get a reaction from a congregation that was sluggish. A question asking, 'Isn't that right?' would evoke an answering 'Amen!' and 'Preach it!' But so would any reference to the cross or the blood of Jesus. He said 'I know how to rouse the people.'

I wonder how you react to this appeal in one of William Booth's letters. He is writing to his fiancée (later wife) Catherine Mumford asking her for sermon ideas:

I want a sermon on the Flood, one on Jonah, and one on the Judgement. Send me some bare thoughts; some clear outlines. Nothing moves the people like the terrific. They must have hell-fire flashed before their faces, or they will not move. Last night I preached a sermon on Christ weeping over sinners, and only one came forward, although several confessed to much holy feeling and influence. When I preached about the harvest and the wicked being turned away, numbers came. We must have that kind of truth which will move sinners.[6]

Words are our trade. Which means that we are always just inches away from manipulation, whether that's dragging in a reference to the cross to raise the emotional temperature or frightening the hesitant into the kingdom with a little judicious fire and brimstone. But the realities to which the words point – the blood of Christ and the judgement of God – are too holy to be spoken of casually.

And what impression is given of the Word of God and the calling of the preacher by the young minister who strolled into the pulpit and said: 'Well, what I'm to say to you this morning God only knows'? Behind the words lies the assumption: 'I'm a professional. I can touch the ark and not get burned.' I hope someone had a go at him afterwards.

Robert Pagliari presses the point home: 'A preacher who rises from prayer and enters a pulpit without trembling at the thought of this responsibility has not prayed. A preacher who speaks without any fear is a gifted orator, a skilful technician, a clever actor, or a colorful parrot, but not really a preacher.'[7]

## THE PERSON IS THE MESSAGE

There is a very moving passage at the end of the letter to the Galatians. For verse after verse Paul has fought against the distortion of the gospel that he found in the Galatian churches. He has used every weapon in his armoury. At the close of the letter, you can almost hear the sigh of weariness as he writes: 'From now on let no one make trouble for me; for I carry the marks of Jesus branded on my body' (Galatians 6.17). Paul's body was a map of his missionary journeys: 'This scar here on the arm, the weals on my back, the limp I'll carry for the rest of my life – you can trace my sermons in Antioch, Iconium and Lystra; each one carried a price tag.' Would anyone doubt that the words matched the life?

In Richard Ward's words: 'As you speak you would like to become a witness to the incarnation, so that God's spirit would become flesh through the "words of your mouth and the meditation of your heart". You would like to be transparent to God's spirit, a prism for God's bright and colourful presence. Every preacher longs for greater transparency in the pulpit.'[8]

How can we respond to this yearning? Perhaps the first move is to confront the dangers set out above. In other words, to strive with God's help to ensure that life and word are congruent, that prayer has soaked the sermon, that we honestly try to say what is true (even if it's awkward or unsensational) and that we use our craft responsibly, not playing on people's guilt, fear or sentimentality but recognizing their freedom, dignity and infinite worth in God's eyes.

But then what? Of the thousands of things that could be said about the integrity and transparency of the preacher, I want to pick out three as embodying the Word in a distinctive way.

## FIRE AND PASSION

Jeremiah complains: 'If I say, "I will not mention him or speak any more in his name", then within me there is something like a burning fire shut up in my bones; I am weary with holding it in, and I cannot' (Jeremiah 20.9). Martyn Lloyd-Jones makes an entertaining comment on this verse. He once heard a preacher expound the text in such a detached way that, as he puts it, the 'one big thing that was entirely missing was *fire* . . . The good man was talking about fire as if he was sitting on an iceberg.'[9] A few pages further on Lloyd-Jones bursts out: 'What is preaching? Logic on fire! . . . It is theology on fire . . . Preaching is theology coming through a man (*sic*) who is on fire.'[10]

W. E. Sangster was another pulpit giant. Once he was interviewing a ministerial candidate who admitted that he was shy and quiet, and would probably never set the Thames on fire. Sangster responded: 'I'm not interested to know if you can set the Thames on fire. What I want to know is this: if I picked you up by the scruff of the neck and dropped you into the Thames, would it sizzle?'[11]

The electrifying effect of preaching with fire and passion is caught by John Wesley when describing a woman testifying: 'While a poor woman was speaking a few artless words out of the fullness of her heart, a fire kindled and ran, as flame among the stubble, through hearts of almost all that heard; so, when God is pleased to work, it matters not how weak and mean the instrument.'[12] It's a pity that Wesley had to be disparaging about the woman, but we see the point he is making. The key to the story is the phrase: 'the fullness of her heart'. We want to know, understandably, how we can catch fire. Self-ignition sounds tricky and we suspect people would see its artificiality. Can the fire be encouraged? If we stand in a certain place will it fall and consume us? Is this fire the same as the 'anointing' of which Martyn Lloyd-Jones made so much?

Well, it seems as if Wesley did identify the fire among the stubble as the anointing power of the Spirit. But he clearly related it to the fullness of the heart, or the passion with which the woman spoke. God may or may not see fit to give us tongues of flame – that is his prerogative – but perhaps there's something we can do as well.

First, it is worth asking myself what it is about God, Christ and the Christian life which gives me a buzz, excites me or stirs me inside. Where does my personal theology, no doubt impeccably orthodox, come alive, where does it spark and fizz? Has it to do with the dance of the Trinity? Or the suffering God? Or the renewing Spirit? Or the amazing and unbelievable grace of Christ? Search for the points at which the spark arcs across the gap between the creed and your heart and let that truth set you on fire. Put bluntly, does anything about God excite you, or has everything gone stale and tired?

Second, look at the particular passage on which you have to preach. At some point an idea in the passage must touch my heart and make me jump or I'm in trouble. Jerry Camery-Hoggatt speaks of the 'Aha' of the passage and the 'Aha' of the sermon. On the road to Emmaus Jesus took old truths, reframed them, gave them a new twist and a fresh application. Reflecting on the experience, the disciples remembered that their hearts had burned as he kaleidoscopically mixed prophecy and law and present experience and brought forth something new and exhilarating. We are looking for the moment when our hearts burn within us. W. E. Sangster said that every preacher should climb the stairs into the pulpit saying under his or her breath, 'Let me get at 'em.' At what point in your reading of the passage do you say, 'Yes!'

Third, rethink your personal image of the preacher's role. Thomas Long likens the preacher to an explorer who goes into the cave, makes an exciting discovery and returns to the congregation crying 'Look what I've found!'[13] This view of preaching encourages us to preach out of the excitement of discovery. We want to share what we have seen. We are personally involved. We bear witness to a truth which has become real for us. How can we not preach with passion?

Finally, follow the advice given to black preachers, 'Pray yourself hot!' Authentic passion, as opposed to synthetic shouting and stomping around, comes as we open ourselves to the Spirit. It demands a willingness to be open before God and to be open in the pulpit. This will entail speaking from the heart. I have seen preachers dutifully following their text suddenly come alive before my eyes. The text is laid aside, they begin to preach fluently, unselfconsciously, wholly engaged with the message which has gripped them. And with the passion comes what the New Testament calls *parrhesia*, the freedom of speech and confidence which overwhelms them and gives them eloquence. 'Pray yourself hot.'

Two final comments. When I refer to passion I do not necessarily mean shouting. Different people show passion in different ways. We can sense when someone is gripped by the Word and speaking personally and with an intensity which comes from the heart. The volume may rise, but equally it may not.

Second, I take the anointing of which Lloyd-Jones and Wesley spoke to be a gift of God, the renewing power of the Spirit which gives preachers the sense that God is owning the words they speak, owning them as his messengers and empowering what they say. The wind blows and catches the sails. It blows where it will; we cannot click our fingers and have it on demand. But we can open ourselves to the possibility, and what I have written above is one way of doing so.

---

**EXERCISE**

*As I write this chapter I anticipate having to preach on the parable of the sower (Matthew 13.1–23) in about six weeks' time. My heart is in my boots. Children's addresses from the past parade before my eyes – involving fictional characters like Luke Warm, Mark Time and Percy Vere. But at this moment the parable feels tired, stale and hackneyed. What possible excitement can I find in there? How would you handle this parable? Where's the buzz and the fizz for you?*

---

## STILLNESS AND SILENCE

This summer I visited Winchester Cathedral. In the crypt I came across a piece of sculpture. It is a solitary, standing figure, set well back into the crypt behind a barrier so that those who enter can't get near but have to view it from a distance. In the shadows, the figure stands silently, looking downwards at a mirror which it holds in its hands. A notice tells me that the crypt floods regularly, but it is now midsummer and I am left having to imagine the figure there in winter, in the dark when the tourists have gone, up to the knees in water, still looking into the mirror. I cannot quite grasp why that figure had such an impact upon me, but I suspect that it was because it spoke to me as a preacher. In a world of words and noise, the sculpture symbolizes withdrawal into the still, silent place where the noise stops. In that still centre the figure sees a true reflection in the mirror and is open to the silence of God.

Speaking practically, what might this image mean for us? Here are a few possibilities. First, we should find a space where we can be quiet in God's presence. We ought also to try to ensure that we spend as much time listening to God as we do talking, a piece of advice which I have read in many books, firmly believe to be vital and still find very difficult to put into practice. Again, in our reading of scripture we shouldn't study only the passage set for the next sermon. The aim is to be still in God's presence, not come up with bright ideas for section 3. In our general reading, we might try to cover less ground but read more attentively and in greater depth. Nor should we limit ourselves to prose. The beauty of reading poetry is that it compels you to take time, to think about individual words and phrases, to let images work on the imagination and to look at life from a new perspective. I would add that, in a busy world, it is no sin to waste time. I remember one minister telling me that, when he was on retreat, he sat in the garden just watching a bird (one bird!) for what seemed like 30 minutes. We might be inclined to react, 'What a waste of time.' But being attentive to detail, being receptive to the world around us without constantly trying to mould it, understand it, categorize it and make it work for us is a soul-restoring thing to do, especially for those who believe that the Word became flesh. The sermon is written in that still and silent place, long before the commentaries are opened, the structure planned or the words crafted. What gets preached is the preacher, and the still place is the place where the preacher is formed.

I don't want to minimize the strain of this. When a sermon is due, I want to get on and put something down on paper. I am relieved when I pick up a good quotation from the paper, or a joke comes from a friend through e-mail, or a lucky visit to an Internet site gives me an idea. The need to say something overwhelms me. If I am not careful then I can drown in words but not hear the Word God wants to say to me. I can easily forget that God wants to speak to me not in order that I should have something to say but in order to make me into the kind of person who can say it. There is a price to be paid in sitting quietly and listening. It has to do with relinquishing control over my sermon. I can no longer cut corners, or just get on, or settle for a superficial hearing of the text or detach the words I speak from the person I am.

Ben Campbell Johnson and Andrew Dreitcer tell a story which powerfully illustrates the strain of waiting on God in silence but which also holds within it something of the promise.[14] During a period of spiritual dryness, a Christian whom they term 'a serious seeker' decides to practise *lectio divina* through the whole New Testament. He begins with the opening verses of Matthew's genealogy – not, one would have thought, the most promising starting place. The material seems at first to offer him nothing. During the third week (and the third verse!) he questions what in heaven's name he is doing with such a deadly passage. But in the middle of the fourth week of 'begats', ploughing on through the list of fathers, he is arrested by the thought that he has spent most of his life wishing he'd never had a father. That revelation leads him to serious exploration of his relationship with his father, his children and with God. 'The boring texts' force him to face the truth. As he slowed down and spent time in the presence of God, God was able to address an issue deep below the surface and eventually to change him.

## LOVE AND COMPASSION

Karl Barth said: 'Preachers must love their congregations. They must not want to be without them. They have to realize: I am part of them, and I want to share with them what I have received from God. It will not help to speak with the tongue of either men or angels if this love is missing.'[15]

It is not always the case that we love the people to whom we speak. Sometimes the sermon is just a chore and the best time of the week is supper time on Sunday with our duty done and the burden lifted for a day or seven. Sometimes we don't much like the people we preach to and then a fiery word of judgement settles a few scores and offloads some irritation. Sometimes we feel the burden of having to represent God and the Church and play the role of ministry spokesperson. 'Why should it always be me who has to explain why earthquakes happen and children die of hunger?' But Barth was right. It will not help to speak with the tongue of either men or angels if love is missing.

Love will show itself in the sermon in countless ways, but according to Calvin Miller it will be seen especially in what he terms 'the integrity of delivery'.[16] The preacher takes his or her stand on four principles which are communicated through the sermon: I am what I appear to be; I trust you to choose for yourself; I respect your dignity and worth; I appreciate your attendance at my sermon and this church. Miller observes that the listeners have 'given me a rather priceless gift – time from their busy lives'. That is why he wants his sermon to be marked by a spirit of appreciation.

In a passionate passage Walter Burghardt links the person of the preacher and the impact of the message:

> Ultimately I am the word, the word that is heard . . . Because I am in love: with the things of God, with the people of God, with God himself. Because the hungers of God's family are my hungers: when they bleed, I weep. Unless some of this breaks through, the word may indeed be proclaimed, but it will hardly be heard.[17]

In all this I am not trying desperately to communicate passion, stillness and love. To attempt to do so would be an artificial exercise and one which would call my integrity into question. I pursue these qualities and persevere in the quest in the faith that this is what a preacher should be like. I don't focus on myself in order that I should be an effective speaker of sermons. I concentrate on myself in the presence of God because that is what I ought to do. It is the heart of my devotion, my identity and my discipleship. Yet, as I seek God's face, I trust that he will so change me that, without my conscious effort, something of that renewed person will be caught and sensed by those to whom I speak.

# 3 This is my story

*Personal disclosure and the preacher*

I remember a while back realizing that I had questions about God that I'd never really got to grips with or given enough thought to and my answers were still the same ones that I'd had in Sunday School. And I suddenly realized 'that won't do'. Those Sunday School answers didn't satisfy me any more. They weren't good enough. I'd got stuck at a certain phase and if I didn't move on I was in real danger of deciding it was all rubbish and I might as well give up. So, it was a bit of a crisis moment. It was quite scary at the time.[1]

June 1980: went to another church meeting, they asked me how I was feeling. I said, 'I threw up eight times today, once in the shower.' People looked at me rather funny, someone said, 'The first item on the agenda tonight is . . .' I have no idea what it was, for I was too embarrassed about being an unseemly part of the Body of Christ.[2]

Like many of you, I've gone through surgery. What an ordeal! Yet even after the bright prognosis and a clean bill of health, I felt a great sense of 'But you promised.' My body should have worked. My arm, my liver, my kidney, my uterus – it should have worked, according to the medical journals and books. And if not, why couldn't I go to a doctor and get it fixed? To remove it was so final. Now it will never work because it's gone. Anger. Guilt. Blame. Sadness. And finally, goodbye.[3]

What is your reaction to these three stories? In a book about embodying the Word, the personal anecdote which illustrates the gospel through some event in the preacher's life would seem to have considerable potential. When people tell their own stories abstract faith becomes real. Surely we would want to commend those preachers who tell stories about themselves?

Not all would agree. The use of personal illustrations has become a subject of intense debate among homileticians. Some experts on preaching have gone so far as to prohibit all personal stories in the pulpit. They see them as bombs waiting to explode in the preacher's face. Is there any middle ground between these two positions?

I begin with an obvious point: preaching involves people speaking and people listening. This cannot be avoided. I suppose it is just possible to prepare the message 'objectively' (whatever that means), keep yourself out of it as much as possible and then photocopy it for the congregation to read. I have attended conferences where learned papers have been read to delegates who have sat with the printed text, turning the page in time with the 'speaker'. But conference papers are not sermons. Sermons get preached by people.

So whether we like it or not, the message will be filtered through the preacher's experience, personality type, understanding of the gospel, views of God, sense of humour, gender and culture. And most of this will have happened before the congregation hears a word.

We can add a second point, as obvious as the first: the person of the preacher will always affect the *reception* of the message. Once the preacher begins to speak, the listeners will get to work with their own filtering, interpreting (and distorting) of the words. The message they take home will be affected in no small measure by their evaluation of the preacher.

## MAKING A GOOD IMPRESSION

At this juncture it may be helpful to introduce a distinction which is often drawn between the *preacher's real character* (i.e. the preacher in the presence of God) and the *preacher's perceived character* (i.e. the preacher as perceived by the congregation – its assessment of his or her character). The preceding chapter explored the idea of the preacher's real character. However, the way a preacher is heard and hence his or her credibility in the congregation's eyes probably relates much more to the preacher's perceived character. Put crudely, if I don't like a preacher I am less inclined to hear the Word of God through them. If I don't think they model the gospel or are trustworthy then I will not trust their words.

What contributes to perceived character? We might pick out the preacher's reputation and the congregation's pre-knowledge as key elements. The preacher comes with academic and spiritual credentials – this is Doctor so and so, the author of twelve books, minister at the Church of Perpetual Revival, beloved conference speaker, whose congregation counts itself 'greatly blessed'. Maybe the preacher's track record is known as well. This is the preacher who missed a funeral, never visited me in hospital, gabbles the wedding service, refused to baptize my grandchild. Or alternatively, was wonderful with my mother when she was dying, is good with teenagers, stayed with me all night in A and E. Something of the reputation spills over into the sermon and affects the hearing.

What happens to perceived character when the preacher is unknown to listeners? The world of first impressions can be the happy hunting ground of stereotypes and prejudices. With little in the way of fact to go on, the listeners are thrown back on generalizations. Irrelevant matters become important: gender; appearance and dress; voice and manner (confident or overbearing); social class (snobbish or working class); ivory tower academic, 'not from round here', funny accent; uses PowerPoint. The manner of taking the service or preaching will affect evaluation. Someone said to me of a nationally famous preacher, 'He's like a duvet, he envelopes you with goodwill and amiability.' Another preacher might be seen as having 'an air of quiet authority' or 'a good sense of humour'. As the real person is slowly cooked through the congregation's prejudices and preferences, the preacher may be judged because he or she reminds individuals of someone else. Unconsciously some in the congregation may see a woman preacher as 'my mother' or 'my daughter' and respond accordingly.

I make these obvious points only to emphasize one function of personal disclosure in the pulpit. A congregation that knows you (and likes you) will make allowances. A strange congregation can jump to conclusions which are unwarranted. The personal story or the joke at the very beginning often has little to do with the sermon. Its true function is to say: 'I'm all right. I'm one of you really. Give me a chance.' It aims to create space for the message. But *all* personal revelations will contribute to the sum total of the preacher's perceived character, whether he or she is known to the congregation or not. It probably only takes a dozen sermons for people to acquire a detailed dossier on the preacher. It may be wise to bear this in mind.

## I REMEMBER A TIME WHEN . . .

One reaction to the terrifying thought that congregations can read us like an open book every time we speak is to ban personal anecdotes. Why give hostages? On the other hand communicating the gospel through personal revelations, the anecdotes which express something of who you are, must surely put flesh on abstract declarations. An observation by James Feehan corroborates this claim. Commenting on a survey carried out by the Irish Liturgical Commission, he notes that 'what the majority of young people wanted to hear in the homily was the preacher's own story of faith'.[4] Feehan commends personal disclosure as relevant to authenticity, vulnerability and grace experience. The preacher as 'wounded healer brings an extra dimension of authenticity'. Well, which is it to be? Are we to be cautious or enthusiastic?

Here is a sample list, all taken from the same preacher:

- Yesterday I was on the Internet and I did what Rick Warren did – I looked up on Amazon.com, that giant online bookstore, every book that had the word 'passion' in the title. There were hundreds and hundreds of books. I narrowed it down to just the 625 titles with 'a passion for' in the title.

- I remember J. John speaking on 'You can't get a camel through the eye of a needle' and saying 'Oh yes, you can – if you liquidize it – though even then the hairs probably get stuck.'
- I rang my wife and said, 'I've had an accident but I'm fine.' I said it the wrong way round. Because she heard the bad news which came first before she heard the good news.
- So there I was, smugly looking at a traffic jam on this highway in Los Angeles far below me and to my right. I was all right. Then I saw the sign marked A100 South and I needed to go north. I joined the slip road; it went round in a long U-turn and, lo and behold, I ended up joining the snarled-up traffic jam. So much for being smug. Grace demands that we stop feeling smug and make a U-turn.
- I received a sample credit card this week – it was a card with the corner cut off – and it offered me more credit. What an interesting comment on our society and money! The automatic assumption everyone makes is that we all need more credit.
- I remember clearing out my mother's house; she had lived 47 years in the same house. The council cleared out the big stuff. Then I found myself standing with my sister on the pavement, surrounded by 63 black bin-liners full of stuff, and thinking, 'That's it, is it?'

I have chosen these six examples because I think, in the context of the sermon, they worked. How might we categorize them? Some don't seem like personal comments at all, for example, the joke about the camel. The Internet reference portrays the preacher as normal and not a Luddite and introduces a section on passion in faith. The stories of the accident and the credit card relate to human nature and our culture. One example consists of an analogy illustration unpacking the concept of repentance as 'turning round'. The black bin-liners touch on a universal experience of feeling the pointlessness of life; even though it's an individual's experience it has a representative quality about it. Taken together, they illustrate something of the variety of functions performed by personal stories.

# SUPERGLUE, VACUUM CLEANERS AND
# UNEXPLODED BOMBS

What are the objections to using personal illustrations? The following points are often made by those who see little but danger:

1   They will stick like glue to the preacher but not to the idea which they illustrate. Congregations will remember the story because personal stories are interesting. They will forget the point of the story.

2   They seldom help congregations to generate similar experiences from their own lives.

3   They may give the impression that personal confidences are being used as illustrations. If the congregation sees the preacher as vacuum cleaner, hoovering up people's pain in order to fill the sermon dust bag, then it feels demeaned. Buttrick comments with some asperity: 'Who would turn to a blabbermouth for counselling?'[5]

4   They run the risk of pandering to the preacher's self-indulgence. We can all fall into the trap of assuming everyone will find our lives intensely interesting.

5   They run the risk of boring the congregation. Too many personal stories are like too many holiday snaps, especially when they harp on and on about the new baby or children or pets or football teams or the holiday in Israel.

6   They may present the preacher as hero. People feel uneasy when a story leaves them with the sense that the preacher has emerged with a considerable amount of credit. This is especially so if the surface text of the illustration is supposed to glorify God. Beware of stories which begin: 'So, there I was, with the Archbishop of Canterbury on one side and the Pope on the other . . .'

7   Conversely, they may present the preacher as victim. The preacher plays a dangerous game when the story expresses too much personal pain and failure. Kind-hearted congregations will want to offer therapy.

8   They may provide more information than the congregation feels it needs. Detailed descriptions of operations, body odour or Athlete's Foot are seldom central to the message.

9   They may inadvertently privilege a whole value system which can distract attention from the purpose of the sermon. An anecdote drawn from family life may carry the implied message: 'Family life with kids is the ideal. Too bad you're not married and don't have kids.'

These objections make uncomfortable reading, especially since personal disclosures are one of the commonest forms of illustration. More positively, we can use the list to construct a code of good practice for self-disclosure. It might run something like this:

- A personal story ought to be honest and truthful, with the temptation to exaggerate and overdramatize firmly resisted.
- It should be ethically and pastorally responsible, neither disparaging people nor patronizing them nor betraying a confidence nor using their distress merely as a sermon illustration.
- Stories which illustrate a universal experience, common to humanity, are helpful since they belong to the congregation as much as to the preacher.
- Personal testimony should aim to be representative rather than purely autobiographical, to be mirrors of the congregation's experience rather than windows into the preacher's personal life.
- Stories which primarily appeal for sympathy have no place in the pulpit.
- Personal stories will always tend to be memorable, and this should be borne in mind in case they overwhelm the point they are intended to illuminate.
- If you think you can glorify yourself and God at the same time, you can't.

---

**EXERCISE**

*Ask a member of your family if you harp on about something all the time.*

---

All this leaves me with the uneasy feeling that there must be more to be said. Identifying reasons why one should not reveal oneself in the sermon seems a pretty negative and rather grudging activity. In his sermon 'Our God is able' Martin Luther King tells the personal story of a time when he received a death threat and of the night of depression which followed.[6] Yet in the morning he found hope renewed and strength to continue the struggle for civil rights. The sermon is the richer as a result. Is it enough to emphasize the perils of self-disclosure without also acknowledging its power?

Those who see value in personal revelation make the point that you can't help revealing yourself however much you try, and therefore you may as well do so with careful forethought and deliberation. Calvin Miller remembers a deacon who would always pray: 'Lord, hide our preacher behind the cross and let us see only Jesus in him.'[7] Miller comments: 'I don't know how well God answered his prayers since I have never felt very well hidden in the pulpit but rather far too exposed and exhibitionist.' Self-disclosure is powerful and inevitable, so we should not use it casually, or as a cheap way of getting an emotional response or because we are too idle to work at other ways of illustrating our message.

Moreover, cutting out all self-disclosure creates its own problems. If we give the impression of deliberately concealing who we are, people think: 'Come out from behind the mask.' A safe and depersonalized message invites the retort: 'Get off the fence, professor.' The image of the preacher as herald can imply (I think wrongly) that the message can be passed on in the style of a public bulletin: 'Speaking on behalf of the council, a spokesperson said . . .' But people do not want a faceless pronouncement. The desperate cry of their hearts is often more like: 'Tell us how it is for *you!*'

Used rightly, self-disclosure embodies the Word. Kasemann said: 'The world is not interested in a Christianity which is an abstraction.'[8] There is a long and noble tradition in Christianity of bearing witness, acknowledging Christ before the world. 'One thing I do know, that though I was blind, now I see.'[9] The importance of personal testimony runs right through the New Testament. Paul tells his story twice in the Acts of the Apostles and the epistles are full of personal disclosures.[10]

Speaking out of personal experience will reveal something of the preacher's humanity. The danger of standing six feet above contradiction is that you can sound as if you are high above the rest of the common herd. Disciplined personal disclosure undercuts the false impression that you are the perfect Christian and that the life of faith is easy for you. Bruce Salmon says: 'The best help we can offer is our own woundedness and a description of what has saved and healed us.' This insight is put dramatically by Tim Keel, a pastor in Kansas City:

> Sports writer Red Smith once said, 'It's really very easy to be a writer; all you have to do is sit down at the typewriter and open a vein.' Likewise it's easy to be a preacher; all you have to do is stand in front of your people and open your vein. But that requires discernment and vulnerability. There are, of course, appropriate levels of disclosure. For unhealthy people, a pulpit can be a dangerous place to work out your issues. A congregation is not a place to do public therapy. You never share anything that you yourself have not significantly reckoned with, especially regarding sexuality.[11]

Perhaps there is one area where it is particularly important that the received orthodoxy which argues against personal disclosure in the pulpit should be resisted. A modest but growing body of research suggests that personal disclosure is a favoured strategy in women's preaching. Cheryl Sanders reports: 'Testifying was the one homiletical task which showed the greatest discrepancy between men and women; only one man out of eighteen offered personal testimony in his sermon, yet eight out of eighteen women did so in theirs.'[12] Heather Walton and Susan Durber also note that 'women are likely to speak more directly from the personal, to name experience in the pulpit which we have previously been told not to name.'[13] If this is so, it constitutes another of the many benefits to the Church of the increase in the number of women preaching and represents a gift which should not be suppressed or disparaged. If women characteristically turn to lived experience when preaching, then 'when a woman who is a role model testifies to the divine, enabling grace at work in her own life and ministry, her successors learn to claim its sustaining power for themselves'.[14] Not only so; as men hear women speaking powerfully and persuasively in this mode they too are encouraged to explore its possibilities for themselves.

There is a wonderful example of preaching oneself in a God-centred way in some words of C. H. Spurgeon:

> I have known what it is to use up all my ammunition, and then
> I have, as it were, rammed myself into the great gospel gun, and I
> have fired myself at my hearers: all my experience of God's
> goodness, all my consciousness of sin, and all my sense of the power
> of the gospel. And there are some people upon whom that kind of
> preaching tells when nothing else does, for they see that then you
> are communicating to them not only the gospel, but yourself also.[15]

Our society is chary of authoritarian modes of communication and looks askance at truth hurled like a stone. Testifying invites hearers to engage with tiny pieces of real life and see if they fit experience. It can flesh out abstract notions like discipleship, penitence, doubt, discernment and show these concepts operating in lived situations. It can inspire people with the possibilities of the life of faith and strengthen them to keep going in hard times. Testifying illustrates the multi-coloured grace of God in human lives, it shows how God is at work in individuals and holds out a promise that, as the song says, 'What He's done for others, He can do for you.' Most important of all, it can bear a rich witness to the preciousness of Christ, the pearl beyond price, and the glory of God expressed in a human being fully alive.

# 4 Swallowing the scroll

## Scripture and the imagination

I had asked a group of trainee preachers to look at the story of Jesus and the leper in Mark 1.40–45 and see what struck them about the passage. They were just starting to offer insights and reactions to the text. As I was looking for the next contribution I noticed that one of them looked preoccupied and I began to wonder if the exercise was too demanding. Then she held out her hand and said, 'I was just trying to imagine what it would be like to see your skin becoming whole after it had been diseased for so long.'

The theme of this chapter is that the Word is more likely to be embodied in our preaching if it has first been embodied in our imaginations. Seeing your diseased skin gradually (or instantaneously) changing into healthy flesh is an example of one way of encountering the biblical text. It's clear that the woman who sat looking at her hand was entering the story rather than sitting outside it.

This is not to disparage analytical methods of understanding a Bible passage. Most books on preaching list *Approaches to Exegesis* which the preacher is recommended to employ at the beginning of the process of sermon construction. For example, Paul Scott Wilson sets out 19 questions to be tackled as you make 'an initial literary reading of a biblical text'. Reassuringly, he promises that 'in time and with patience and experience the process will become easier and more automatic'.[1] Stephen Farris offers 'a brief exegetical method' which consists of ten main questions with numerous sub questions.[2] In *A Preaching Workbook* I could not resist adding to the heap of good advice, setting out a checklist of eight tasks.[3] All such lists have their uses, and the analytical method is an indispensable tool in encouraging the Bible to yield up its treasures.

However, there is little to be gained by revisiting ground that has been admirably covered in many other studies. Nor do I want to set one approach against another in an artificial polarization. My aim in this chapter is a limited one. I want to explore methods which help preachers to experience the Bible imaginatively.

At the outset, it is best to be clear about the role of imagination in encountering the Bible. Barbara Brown Taylor puts it beautifully:

> Imagination has no point to make, no axe to grind. It is more like a child roaming the neighbourhood on a free afternoon, following first the smell of fresh bread in an oven, then the glint of something bright in the grass – led by curiosity, by hunger, by hope, to explore the given world from its highest branches to its deepest roots because it is wonderful and terrible and because it is there. When imagination comes home and empties its pockets, of course there will be some sorting to do. Keep the cat's-eye marble, the Japanese beetle wing, the red feather, the penny. Jettison the bottle cap, the broken glass, the melted chocolate stuck with lint. But do not scold imagination for bringing it all home or for collecting it in the first place.[4]

The time will come for analysis and evaluation. Not everything that pops into our minds ought to find its way into the sermon. People are often overanxious that the Bible may turn into a kind of ink-blot test, its straightforward meaning suppressed as we give full rein to our hang-ups, preferences and daydreams. In fact, I think there's more danger that the reverse will happen and the disapproving right half of the brain will not allow us to cosy up to the text. A friend of mine said with some asperity: 'Even the soaps get us going in a way the Bible doesn't. When they open the Bible, po-faced woodenness descends on otherwise intelligent people.' Strong stuff! At present we don't need to worry about being too imaginative. But, in any case, our reading of any passage needs to be supplemented and disciplined by other methods of exegesis.

## LIVING IN THE STORY

The first method I want to look at has been around for about 500 years. In the sixteenth century Ignatius of Loyola developed a system of exercises designed to nourish spiritual growth. Many Christians today use Ignatian meditation in their own devotional Bible reading, but it seems to me that it can profitably be used when a preacher is trying to get to grips with a text.

Behind the method is the assumption that 'biblical narrative is story – not that it did not happen, but that we need to enter into it as story, into the lives of the characters and the unfolding of the scene, and find our own place there'.[5] The first stage is to take time to contemplate the scene in one's mind's-eye. As Ignatius put it: 'To view with the eyes of the imagination the synagogues, towns and villages through which Christ our Lord went preaching' (p. 25)[6] or 'To view the place or cave of the nativity, how large or small it was, and how high and low it was, and what it was like inside . . . to see people, that is, to see our Lady and St Joseph and the maid servant, and the infant Jesus after he is born . . .' (p. 29). This is the stage of contemplation.

The second move consists of conversation (or dialogue or colloquy). Here the reader enters the story and becomes an actor in the scene. Ignatius says of the Stable meditation: 'I minister to them in their need as if I were present there with the utmost respect and reverence. Then I reflect about myself in order to derive some benefit' (p. 29). The degree of involvement is illustrated by the following suggestion: 'The colloquy is made as when a friend speaks to a friend, or a servant to his master, asking sometimes for some grace, and at other times accusing oneself about one's evil deeds and on other occasions making known one's own affairs and seeking counsel about them' (p. 17). Ignatius realized how powerful a technique this was and recommended that it should be carried on into daily life. So sharing a meal with Christ in the pages of the gospel develops into eating with Christ in one's home. 'As he eats his food let him do so as if he was in the presence of Christ our Lord eating with his disciples. See how Christ drinks, looks and speaks . . .' (p. 51).

Charles Rice makes the connection between this kind of meditation and the sermon which may result: 'If we have an experience of the text, allow ourselves to be led deeply into its images – in our mind's eye to see its people, places, and things – to experience its language as a new dawning, there is every likelihood that the resulting sermon will in form and content, rely upon and awaken the imagination.'[7]

The kind of preaching which results from Ignatian meditation can be illustrated by this excerpt:

The gospels are full of pictures; they come to us as still lifes but they are waiting to move and through them Christ will meet us again and again. At the end of Luke's gospel there is a freeze frame of Jesus which never ceases to stir me (Luke 24.40–43). It catches a simple action, mundane, earthly, grossly materialistic, almost banal. The disciples in the upper room think Jesus is a ghost and he asks them, 'Have you got anything to eat?' Where have you heard that before? It's the cry of the ravenous teenage son – 'What's in the fridge?' The disciples say, 'We've just had supper but there's a bit of broiled fish'. And he eats it in front of them.

And here I am confronted with a Jesus who is real, in my kitchen, as it were. There he stands, just to the right as you stand at the sink, leaning against the Savannah working surface, next to the toaster. It's a Jesus who walks into my living room asking, 'What CDs have you got?' A Jesus seated at the dinner table, laughing, and saying 'The *crème brulee* is fantastic.' Or sitting in the passenger seat of the car saying, 'Are you worried about this appointment?' Or walking with me as I go to a difficult meeting and reassuring me with the words, 'I've been here before you and prepared the way.'[8]

## MAKING A FILM

Related to Ignatian meditation is a method which invites us to use all our senses to imagine the biblical scene. Here we do not enter the scene but we try to imagine how we would shoot it if it were a film. This task takes us into camera angles and close-ups. It makes us ask about a soundtrack. It forces us to structure the action: 'Where will the dramatic close-up come?', 'Do I set this to the theme music from *The Aviator* or *Lord of the Rings*?', 'Is the camera panning slowly across the scene or am I, as director, cutting rapidly from face to face?' Read Luke's account of Jesus in Gethsemane (Luke 22.44) and notice the zoom lens move in on Jesus' face as the sweat runs down his face in drops of blood.

Mary's visit to Elizabeth in Luke 1.39–47 has never been the same for me since a workshop where a young minister told the group how she would shoot the scene. I had never appreciated how fast the pace (Mary sets out with haste into the hill country), how energetic the movement (the baby leaps in the womb) and just how noisy it all was (Mary's greeting makes John the Baptist jump and Elizabeth exclaims with a loud cry).

There seems to be a lot of shouting going on. No wonder Mary's *Magnificat* bursts out like champagne when the cork is popped.

Once you have done this exercise it is very difficult not to preach the passage in a multi-sensory manner. You can see the scene in your mind's eye. Voice and gesture will embody what you are looking at as it happens on your mental screen. The great thing about film is that it is a visual medium and so making even an imaginary film will force you into sense impressions. Barbara Brown Taylor, an expert in the area of the imagination, says: 'I have always thought that believers in the word made flesh have an implicit duty to attend to physical details in the language they use. It is not enough to say what something means, without also disclosing how it looks, sounds, smells, tastes and feels. If we can trust those details, then very often the meaning will take care of itself.'[9]

---

### EXERCISE

*Try creating a film script for John 8.1–11, the woman taken in adultery.*

---

## LISTENING TO THE BODY

I came across another memorable phrase of Barbara Brown Taylor – 'a visceral connection with scripture'.[10] 'What does that say to you?' I asked my wife. She said, 'Well, getting scripture in the guts, I suppose.' Connecting with the Bible in an almost physical way will ensure that its message is embodied. The image is a thoroughly biblical one. Ezekiel is commanded to eat the scroll and says, 'In my mouth it was as sweet as honey.' Jeremiah eats God's words and declares, 'They became to me a joy and the delight of my heart.'[11]

Earlier this year, I was working with someone about to preach her first sermon – on the treasure hidden in a field. 'You'd better try to imagine what it's like to trip over a box,' I said, half jokingly. When the time came for her to preach the sermon we watched in fascination as she mimed going for a walk in the country. We felt her stub her toe – ouch! Then we watched her bend and scrabble in the soil. We discovered the box with her, following closely as she tugged at it, pulling it clear with great effort – lots of white knuckles and straining forearms. As I remember it, the box was covered with earth which she brushed off and – oh yes – the clasp was stiff and hard to undo and the lid opened away from her. But inside! Well, I counted at least two necklaces (which she wound round her neck), three rings and dozens of coins which she ran through her fingers. We felt the panic when it dawned on her that the field wasn't hers and shared her urgency as she pushed the box back into the ground, covered it with soil and stamped the earth flat. It was a riveting couple of minutes, and words don't do justice to the experience.[12]

This is not a plea for preachers to become professional mime artists, though I am sure that discipline is highly relevant. Miming part of the scriptural event is a fruitful way of indwelling the text. Thomas Troeger's book *Imagining a Sermon* contains a chapter entitled 'Feel the weight of bodily truth'.[13] He advocates 'walking through' a biblical incident imagining what it feels like, not so much by finding the right words but by letting our bodies teach us through movement. How would I know what it feels like to bow down and worship the Lord unless I do it? How could I get inside the mind of the tax collector better than by standing afar off, not daring to raise my eyes to heaven and beating upon my breast?

Troeger, a little unfortunately, calls this 'logosomatic language', connecting the Greek words for 'word' and 'body'. Much biblical language, he argues, is 'close to the nerve and bone of being human'. One way of accessing it is by acting out the scene or turning the idea into movement.

Walter Wink makes a similar suggestion in a book on different methods of Bible study. He focuses on the passage in Matthew 5.23–24: 'So when you are offering your gift at the altar, if you remember that your brother or sister has something against you, leave your gift there before the altar and go; first be reconciled to your brother or sister, and then come and offer your gift.' Wink advocates: 'Physically walk through the act of bringing your gift (real or imaginary) to the altar and there remember someone who has something against you'.[14] My colleague, Geoffrey Stevenson, uses this incident in sermon workshops. He encourages participants to feel the weight of the gift, to be specific about its nature, and imagine what it cost them. He continues: 'Prepare mentally to take it in, but stop outside the door. Your brother/sister has something against you. Put the package down. Leave it outside the door. Turn and take five or six steps towards where you came from. How easy or hard was it to make that turn?'

Stevenson is clear that doing this exercise will not bring you an Olivier Award. You do it in private, forcing yourself to go past the point of 'I'll look stupid.' But connecting with the action may evoke a fresh understanding of the passage, and that may seep into the sermon.

---

**EXERCISE**

*Try this exercise on the parable of the lost coin. Search for a lost coin or, better, your cash card. Make sure you know exactly why it is urgent that you find it. Is it here in the house or did I leave it somewhere? Will I have to cancel the card? I have to be out of the house ten minutes ago, and tonight's meal isn't bought, and there are people coming. Find it after looking in eight to ten different places. Notice how you feel the relief, and where in your body.*[15]

---

## PERFORMING THE TEXT

My final example of 'embodying methods' was suggested to me when I attended a workshop by Dennis Dewey. Dewey calls himself a biblical storyteller, but this description does not have the usual meaning of someone who freely paraphrases Bible stories and retells them in his or her own words. The definition of his art which appears on his website runs as follows:

> Biblical storytelling is a spiritual discipline which entails the lively interpretation, expression and animation of a narrative text of the Old or New Testament that has first been deeply internalized and is then remembranced, embodied, breathed and voiced by a teller/performer as a sacred event in community with an audience/congregation.[16]

Phrases like 'animation', 'internalized', 'embodied', 'voiced' attracted me to the possibilities of this method. When Dewey speaks of storytelling he envisages someone telling the biblical text in a dramatic fashion but without altering the text. He notes that storytelling is an embodied activity and 'sometimes a story begins in the muscles'.

Having watched and been impressed by Dewey's storytelling I thought I would try it for myself. I did not have a public performance in mind but was more interested in what happened to me in the process of learning a passage by heart and speaking/acting it out. My first experiment was with the stories of Jesus receiving little children, rebuking the disciples and conversing with the rich young ruler in Mark 10.13–22. At first I was obsessed with the difficulty of learning the words until it dawned on me that I was not going to speak the story before an audience, and perfect accuracy wasn't terribly important. As I worked on the passage the need to express and embody the narrative in voice, pauses, gestures and facial expression forced me to internalize the movement and intention of the text. I began to inhabit the story. The 'performance', in the first instance to a bedroom wall, impressed no one but I realized the force of Dewey's advice: 'Do not think in terms of "bringing the story to life" but of finding the life that is already in it.'

I can only recommend that you experiment for yourself. Having to make decisions about the tone of Jesus' words, the shape of the narrative and the postures and expressions of the main actors compelled me to work hard on the text – but in a way which gave my imagination room to move. Having now tried the method on many occasions, I would highlight one of Dewey's insights: 'You learn a lot from inside the story when it is inside you.'

Here are four ways of getting scripture inside you. Some may wonder if the methods will work only with narrative. A lot of the Bible does not take narrative form and the epistles and the psalms in particular seem not to fit easily into the examples I have set out above. However, non-narrative portions of the Bible may still have a story lurking in the background, as it were. A law in Deuteronomy may unveil a community problem as vivid as anything in *Emmerdale*. A psalm may hint at a series of events which has led up to its composition. An epistle often reveals something of the question to which it is an answer. Implied narratives can still respond to the techniques I have outlined. After all, the methods are not a new and improved way of arriving at hitherto unknown exegetical information: they are a way of making a visceral connection with scripture.

Moreover, epistles frequently contain vivid images which are freeze-frames waiting to move. Let them move and bring yourself into the narrative which ensues. Imagine you are studying Colossians 2.13–14 and read:

'the written code, with its regulations, that was against us and that stood opposed to us; he took it away, nailing it to the cross' (NIV). You notice the images and allow yourself to enter the implied story. Then you might find yourself handling the document which contains a record of all your failures, scanning its demands and noting your mistakes. You might find it snatched from you by Christ, who walks away, takes up hammer and nails, and fixes it to the cross. You might see him return to you, take you by the arm and say, 'Leave it hanging there to rot. Come with me, there's a life to be lived. Let's go and live it.'

---

**EXERCISE**

*Learn and speak Matthew 9.18–26.*

---

# 5 The lightning and the thunder

*The preacher and pulpit performance*

A man came – I think it was actually in Philadelphia – on one occasion to the great George Whitefield and asked if he might print his sermons. Whitefield gave this reply; he said, 'Well, I have no inherent objection, if you like, but you will never be able to put on the printed page the lightning and the thunder.'[1]

I have some sympathy with Whitefield. It may seem self-contradictory to *write* about the *delivery* of the sermon. A video would do a better job. But if we are exploring the ways in which preachers embody the Word, then performing can hardly be omitted. As we have seen, all preachers hope that the reality of God will shine through them to some degree; they also know that, used judiciously, their own life experiences can flesh out their message. But they are only too aware that their whole body will be involved in the practical task of communicating what they want to say. Delivery and performance are essential to preaching. In the end a sermon is not a script but an event.

This may be an uncomfortable idea for some. We think of performance as putting on an act. Preachers who strut their stuff on the podium, who weep on cue and put stage directions in the margins of their sermon scripts give preaching a bad name. How much more spiritual to speak the words as undemonstratively as possible so that the pure doctrine can pass directly into the hearts of the listeners, uncontaminated by fleshly striving. Some preaching traditions advocate keeping the lid on anything that might look like enthusiasm. Apparently, John Henry Newman read his sermons in a flat monotone and hundreds flocked to hear him.

It's a nice thought. But it would be naïve to suppose that there is a pure method of communicating which removes the human agent completely. Even when standing absolutely motionless and speaking in a monotone, you will still communicate something, like it or not. In fact, there is a danger that your performance will give off unintended messages like:

'I don't really care much about this or about you', 'This is dull stuff', 'How soon can I get away?' I remember a BBC director saying to me, 'For goodness' sake, smile! You look like you're at a funeral.'

Perhaps we can rescue the idea of 'performing' if we think of performing a piece of music. This may dispel anxieties about artificiality and theatricality. The performer wants the music to be heard, and wants to do justice to the composer's original intention. Giving time, thought and practice to the performance is a way of keeping faith with the piece and its composer. The parallel with preaching is clear. At the most basic level, for instance, it's not unspiritual to make sure that we speak clearly and audibly. It's a mark of respect to the congregation, to the sermon and to God.

## BRINGING THE WORDS OFF THE PAGE

Somehow the words have to be brought off the page. Are there sensible steps we can take to ensure that what we intend to say actually gets said? Books on preaching are full of good advice. I summarize some of the most useful here.

If you are using a full script make sure that, when you write it, you are hearing the words in your head. Otherwise you will end up with a piece which will sound like written English but will lack the rhythms of oral speech. Use direct speech where you can, rather than reported speech, so go for first- and second-person singular. Shorten most of the sentences. Verbs and nouns are stronger than adjectives. Use the active voice rather than the passive. Note the effect of questions, real or rhetorical. Make sure that you mark the transitions from one unit of thought to another. To take a minor example of this principle: though it sounds like preaching by numbers, I have often found it helpful to repeat the opening phrase of a move (if it's functioning as a heading) at the end of the move. It gives a clear signal that I've finished this idea and am now moving on.

Many writers advise preachers to write the text out in short lines, indenting subordinate phrases and using the white space on the page generously. Then, they argue, you will speak the words according to their sense and your eye will come back to the right place on the page. To be sure, it is disconcertingly easy to tell when someone is using a full text, unless they are very skilful at delivering it. More disturbing for the listeners is the experience of watching the speaker move from preaching the words to reading them. You suddenly realize that the preacher has stopped being engaged by the sense of the passage and is going through the motions.

When it comes to the moment of delivery take time to survey the congregation. Don't rush in. Maintain eye contact. Don't preach at the rafters. Avoid the 'slow blink'. Aim for variety in pace, pitch and volume. Don't use a 'pulpit voice'. Pauses and silences can be immensely powerful. Work on the dramatic dimension and try for immediacy in performance. This means becoming a character, miming actions and responses, 'acting all the parts' and, within reason, 'doing all the voices'.

While you are not trying to be an actor, nevertheless appreciate that the message is carried as much by paralinguistic methods as by the actual words. In other words, facial expressions, bodily posture and gestures are worth thinking about and practising beforehand. I was once present at a lecture which was being signed for the deaf. It was a good lecture but the speaker had to compete with the signers at the front. (Sign language really ought to be compulsory for preachers.) The lecturer was talking about St Brendan and his companions setting out in a boat from Ireland, not knowing where they were going and trusting entirely in the wind of the Spirit. The audience was electrified, not so much by the words as by the signer. Before our eyes, she was tossing and turning in the storm and hanging on to the mast for dear life.

I have found two strategies particularly helpful by way of preparation for preaching. First, experiment with lots of different ways of speaking your material. Try the effect of saying the same passage loudly or softly. See what a pause feels like. Mark a transition in an exaggerated way in order to get used to the importance of communicating a clear structure. Practise and experiment.

Second, get someone to listen to you preach before the day itself. I am not sure a close family member is a very good idea, but a friend who will speak the truth is worth much fine gold. Clasp them to you and never let them go. Those in charge of training usually ensure this will happen with new preachers but we tend to be less certain of its value for the experienced. Unfortunately, it is often the preacher who has got into set ways who will benefit most from an honest critique. I realize it will take great grace to submit to such a discipline, but how else will you get feedback before the day? There's nothing so valuable as the comment 'Halfway through I lost you completely', while you still have time to rectify the problem.

Such a lot of advice all in one go is enough to give anyone indigestion. The tension between the preacher who feels 'The Lord's hand is upon me and the fire burns in my bones' and the performer taken up with practising, experimenting and rehearsing may seem irreconcilable. I don't think they necessarily contradict each other, however. God can be honoured in our craft as much as in our spontaneity.

## GIVING AN IDEA WEIGHT

Out of the wealth of principles of good practice which the books offer, I want to concentrate on one theme for the remainder of this chapter. It's a common situation in preaching. The preacher wants to make a number of points but realizes that one is much more important than the others. They are not all on the same level of significance: one needs to stand out.

If a sermon were just a written script, the problem of emphasizing one idea could be dealt with easily. We have a range of markers: texts which are emboldened or italicized will jump off the page; a sub-heading will alert the reader to an important idea; educational text-books may even print the paragraph or statement in larger type.

Oral presentations cannot employ typefaces and italics. It is fascinating to see how often a good sermon fails because the key idea has not been adequately framed and stressed. The preacher may utter the point but not make it count, as it were. The word 'salient' comes from a Latin word which means 'to jump'. That gives us an image to play with. The salient idea needs to leap out at us. At the moment it is behaving like a shy wallflower. No more than an insubstantial wraith, this ghostly figure is almost lost in the crowd of other ideas. It needs a good meal to give it some substance and then to come centre stage, look us boldly in the eye and make its presence felt. If it could jump up and down, shout and wave its arms around we would surely notice it. This calls for the oral equivalent of italics, emboldening and 36-point font size.

So what are the different techniques commonly used to give an idea weight? You might like to try an exercise before we look at some actual sermonic methods.

Now analyse the techniques you used to make your point. It is likely that you tried some at least of the following methods:

- *Repetition:* 'You are not going out looking like that. I'm telling you. You are not going out looking like that.'
- *Paraphrase:* (saying the same old thing in dozens of different ways) 'You are not going out looking like that. Absolutely not. No way. I'm sorry but it's non-negotiable. It's not going to happen.' (Note that these remarks have not moved the discussion along much but they have emphasized the line you are disposed to adopt.)
- *Expansion:* Perhaps you tried expanding the main thought by giving lots of examples. 'Do you know what a dishcloth is? I said "Do – you – know – what – a – dishcloth – is?" A dishcloth is for washing dishes. It is not for wearing in public. What on earth are people going to think when they see you prancing about in a dishcloth?' (The dishcloth example came from a participant at a conference I was taking. It provides a good example of the question which is not concerned with asking for information but is used chiefly to underline a point.)

It is also likely that you used a number of non-verbal methods – dramatic pauses, variations in pace, hand and finger gestures (the jabbing finger and the dismissive wave of the hand). Perhaps you moved incisively so that your whole body added weight to your words (movements probably described as 'stomping about' and 'losing it' by your offspring).

## BRINGING BALLAST ON BOARD

Look at the following excerpt from a sermon on Acts 16, Paul at Philippi. The preacher is making the fair point that the central character, the slave girl who has pursued Paul and Silas through the streets, suddenly disappears from the narrative:

> But, do you know? There was nothing at all in any of my large and erudite tomes about it being a story of silence. The silence of what happened to the slave girl who ceased to be a source of income for those who had exploited her.

The point is made clearly enough but could possibly do with a little more weight. There are many ways of doing this and, before you read on, you might like to try a few for yourself. What, for example, might be the effect of adding some ballast in between the two sentences? Then the paragraph would read like this:

> But, do you know? There was nothing at all in any of my large and erudite tomes about it being a story of silence. Forty-three pages of learned observations and not a word about the main character. It's as if the screen went blank two-thirds of the way through the drama. We ask, 'Excuse me, did I miss something? Run the video back a bit.' But when we do, there's nothing there. Total silence. Not a word. I wonder if you're asking the same question as I am? *What about the girl?* What happened to her? How are we to explain the silence of what happened to the slave girl who ceased to be a source of income for those who had exploited her?

Forty-seven words have turned into 125, but that isn't the main point. This isn't about padding. It's about giving body to a paragraph which introduces a new and important idea.

## REPEATING, PARAPHRASING AND EXPANDING

Repetition, paraphrase and expansion are methods we employ every day in ordinary conversation. Here is a delightful introduction to a sermon on bread by Susan Durber. She gives weight to her point by taking the listeners through many different experiences of bread. The key statement is probably that bread is both ordinary and miraculous and she will play with this idea throughout the rest of the sermon. Here the concept is given weight by looking at it first from one angle and then another and another:

> One of the nice things about travelling away anywhere has to be eating the local bread. Think of French baguettes, fresh and crusty, eaten with good soft cheese and a glass of local wine. Think of German rye bread, malty and strong with almost the texture of cake. Or how about Irish wheaten bread with a tough nutty taste that's all its own? Or there's Italian pizza dough or Jewish matzos or Palestinian pitta filled with falafel, salad and spicy sauce. Or how about chapattis, puri, or nan? Am I making you hungry? Bread is the staple food for many of the world's people and there's such a variety of it. It is one of those things that is at once very ordinary and also miraculous. How, I've always wondered, did it come about that someone discovered what could happen when flour was mixed with yeast and water and a little oil or fat? What a gift to the world! Bread seems to many of us the very basis of life. It even makes it into the prayer we say every day, 'Give us this day our daily bread'. It is both ordinary and miraculous.[2]

An excellent example of emphasizing a key idea comes in this excerpt from a sermon by Geoffrey Stevenson. He wants to stress that the mustard seed in the parable was 'the smallest of all seeds'. This basic and simple idea is approached through repetition, mime, the multiplication of examples and questions to the congregation. Phrase after phrase suggests emphasis through tone and pitch and facial expression. At the end of the paragraph you should have formed the strong impression that the seed was small.

> So here we are, we're looking at a tiny seed. A tiny, tiny, tiny seed – did I say it was small? It is. Very small. Tiny in fact. (The preacher mimes losing it.) As small as a *smile* that you give to someone who in their day so far has only met scorn and indifference . . . as small as a *vote* in a local election . . . as small as *communion* taken to the house-bound elderly . . . as small as an *arrow prayer* in the business of the day . . . as small as . . . you get how small it is. And hidden within this tiny seed are all the information and instructions needed for it to grow – to take some moisture, multiply some cells, and push out a tiny, tiny, tiny tendril. Did I say the tendril was small? It was, at first even smaller than the seed. And it pushes its way *out* into the soil, and *up* into the air, and starts working with the sunlight to produce chlorophyll . . . and that's about the limit of my biology . . .[3]

Of course the paragraph is doing other jobs as well as emphasizing the small size of the mustard seed – the examples which expand the notion of smallness also signal something about the direction of the sermon, and the extension dealing with the tendril contains claims about the power hidden in the seed.

There are four other methods to which I'd like to draw attention. They work in similar ways and rely mainly on not giving away your hand all at once.

## RESCRIPTING THE STORY

Imagine you have to preach on the parable of the Prodigal Son. The difficulty with preaching this parable is that it has been told so many times that the listeners can no longer *feel the force* of the father's gracious reception of the son. We assume that the father will see him afar off, gird up his loins and come running. What could be more obvious? After all, it's a picture of the grace of God, and God will forgive, it's what he's good at. How can we give weight to the idea that the father's response is amazing, far beyond expectation?

45

The most effective method I have ever seen of highlighting the father's
generosity came in a piece of street drama. Because I was in the crowd
watching, I can't remember the exact text but it went something like this.
The son returned to the father and was greeted by: 'If you think I'm going
to have you back after all you've done, you've got another think coming.
You swan off, waste half my money and then come crawling back smelling
of pigswill. Push off!' The son replied plaintively: 'What about repentance?
What about a second chance? What about forgiveness?' The father
retorted, 'What about a bunch of fives?'

Here is the beginning of a sermon on Peter and John at the Beautiful
Gate in Acts 3. It uses the same technique of offering an unexpected
version of the story.

A modern translation of this story runs like this: One day Peter and
John were going up to the temple at the time of prayer – at three in
the afternoon. Now a man crippled from birth was being carried to
the temple gate called Beautiful. When Peter saw him he said to
John, 'Take no notice. It's Reuben the beggar – he's always there.
He's just a scrounger and probably an illegal immigrant. They bring
it on themselves. I wonder what he got up to in a previous life?
Anyway, I've left my wallet at home and I've no small change. Just
wave at him and walk past.' So they went into the temple for 3 p.m.
prayers. And the man? Well, he's still there as far as I know.

## RUNNING THROUGH THE OPTIONS

Let's go back to the parable of the Prodigal Son. We could try to bring out
the force of the father's reaction by an alternative method. This time we
rehearse the thoughts of the prodigal as he stands in the pig sty 'coming to
himself'.

What am I going to do? I've reached the absolute bottom. Even my father's servants have a better deal than I do. I'll go home and throw myself on his mercy. You never know, he may give me a second chance . . . Oh come on, who am I kidding? I insulted him by demanding my half of the property while he was still alive. It was as good as wishing him dead. And he's had to live with the scandal of that all these years. The neighbours all whispering 'Here's the man who couldn't manage his own children.' And if I do go back they'll all watch me as I go through the village, nudging and prodding one another, smirking and waiting to see what my father will do. He was a respectable landowner, pillar of the community, and since I left he's been struggling to live down the shame. With all those eyes on him how can I expect him to lose face and have me back? Do I honestly think he'll let bygones be bygones? Not even if I grovel in the dirt . . .

The preacher gives weight to the main idea by running through alternative possibilities. By presenting us with a range of options, the extraordinary nature of what actually happened is underlined.

---

**EXERCISE**

*It would be a useful exercise to use this technique on the parable of the Good Samaritan. I remember a 14-year-old boy telling me once that he could hardly wait for the day that the Good Samaritan walked over and kicked the man into the ditch. He'd probably heard the story a dozen times in his school life and was now thoroughly bored. Imagine you are the Samaritan at the point where you first catch sight of the injured traveller. Rehearse the different options open to him so as to bring out the astonishing compassion which he showed.*

---

## SPEAKING WITH THE BODY

I mentioned earlier the power of non-verbal or paralinguistic methods of emphasizing key ideas. It is very difficult to illustrate these through the medium of a written text, but to get some idea of the way they work, try 'preaching' the following passage, accompanying the words with movement, gestures, facial expressions and the strategic use of pauses and silence.

> What if she'd said 'No'? What if she's been too busy; or too conventional; or too afraid? There were a hundred ways of getting out of it: 'It's market day', 'I'm not that sort of girl', 'It's the wrong time of the month'.
>
> For a fleeting moment the consequences of saying 'Yes' ran past her; the stranger saw the fear and panic in her eyes and hastened to reassure her. 'Do not be afraid: you have found favour with God.'
>
> Well, God's favour was one thing: an important thing I'm sure and thank you very much; but I've got to go on living in this community, with these particular neighbours, in this particular tight-knit, traditional, hard-working peasant village. I'm not sure that saying 'Yes' to you will find favour with them.[4]

I once heard a meditation on repentance in the chapel of a Franciscan community. Behind the communion table hung an enormous crucifix. The preacher illustrated his point by physically turning his back on the cross and walking away from it. He stopped, still facing away and argued with himself. He half turned back, then paused and turned away again. Finally, he turned completely round, lifted his face towards the figure on the cross and began slowly to return. The effect was electrifying, the words immeasurably enhanced by the physical movement.

## KEEPING THEM DANGLING

It is also worth spending time experimenting with pauses and carefully placed silences. For example, after Paul's encounter with Christ on the way to Damascus, Ananias is sent by God to visit him. In the story in the Acts of the Apostles, Ananias welcomes Paul into the community of Christians with just two words. These two words are obviously highly significant in the context of the whole story. But on their own, they will hardly bear the weight they are being required to carry: so they need to be framed. Try framing them with a dramatic pause before you say them and possibly with a pregnant silence afterwards. This may seem like the worst kind of amateur dramatics, but try it with and without the pause and the silence so as to gauge the effect.

Now add one or two moves which will delay the point further. Give the words weight by taking your time to get to them. Holding back the actual phrase will create suspense and so emphasize it. Perhaps it might come out something like this:

Did I mention the two words Ananias uttered? Did I say what they were? Well, you probably know them but if you don't, I'll tell you – in a minute. Just two words – and with those words Paul is taken to the heart of the little Christian community in Damascus, received by grace and embraced by the gospel. Imagine the scene. Paul sits on a stool, head in his hands, unable to see. He is in turmoil. I know what I would say if I were there. 'Hah, you see, God is not mocked. Serves you right for persecuting Christians. Not so confident now, are we? Eh?' But in fact, none of that happens. Ananias comes in and stands in front of him, stretches out his hands and says . . .

Well, I have delayed the ending for 128 words and I can't keep it up much longer. The two words at the heart of the narrative have got to carry a lot of freight. You might like to try your own way of giving them body. You'll find the text in Acts 9.17.

# PART 2

*The Word embodied in the words*

# 6 Putting people in the picture

*Retelling the Bible story*

They came in their thousands, the whole Rag, Tag and Bobtail of
them. All to the river. To be submerged. It's not easy to say why
they came. Not really a day out with the family. Listening to a
preacher who's all fire and brimstone, with a bit of hell and judgement thrown in. Frighten the kids, upset the dog and wouldn't do a
lot for granny either, what with her being nervous and not specially
partial to being shouted at even when she hadn't got her hearing
aid in. But still they came, noisily, sweatily. Lovers and likely lads.
Coach parties with cans, families with packed lunches, the world
weary, the starry-eyed, those who longed for the beginning of a new
age and those who were just hanging on for the end of today. They
came in droves, as if they were going to the fair or a day out at the
seaside. And with them the pickpockets and the tarts, the soldiers,
narrow eyed, looking for trouble (move along please, the new age
doesn't start here), and the religious people, dying of good taste,
afraid of catching something potentially damaging to health, like
the pox, or the spirit of God.

This is the beginning of a sermon on the baptism of Jesus in Matthew's
Gospel. It represents one of the commonest ways in which we try to
embody the message. We take the biblical story and retell it in our own
words. Sunday School teachers have been doing this for years. In *A
Preaching Workbook* I touched on this method and pointed out the importance of being disciplined by the text so as not to be drawn away into
flights of imaginative fantasy. But I also hinted at the power of this kind of
retelling, especially when the biblical world is allowed to enter our world
and *vice versa*. In this chapter I want to expand on these principles.

Let us begin with the tension between imagination and the text. In the
excerpt set out above, imagination may seem to have gone mad. There is
very little about coach parties in Matthew's account. The preacher could

have stayed firmly within the world of the New Testament. If he had chosen that course then he would have drawn on what the commentaries tell us about the terrain around the Jordan plus such information as we have about popular expectations of a coming messiah during this period. He might have mentioned what we know of apocalyptic preachers and the yearning of an occupied nation for freedom. Commentaries are especially useful on subjects like where wild honey is to be found and the hopes of the Qumran community. It doesn't take long to discover all we would ever want to know about locusts (even that the word ought possibly to be translated *carob beans*).

This would have been a sound approach. It illustrates the value of filling out the biblical account. Biblical stories are pared to the bone. Generally they move too quickly for people to appreciate their force. By elaborating on the bare story the preacher gains space. In that space he can give the story time to work on the imaginations of the listeners and flesh out both detail and meaning. What is more, a fresh retelling helps people hear the familiar story as if for the first time. It produces a new hearing of the Word.

There are a few perils involved, however. The commonest is not missing a chance to display all the hard work you've put into researching the background:

Reuben stood there amazed as Zacchaeus made his announcement. Restoring everything fourfold! This was far beyond what the Jewish law required. Why, restitution in connection with theft only required the addition of a fifth. Even the Romans, with whom Zacchaeus spent so much of his time – filthy collaborator that he was – only asked for fourfold restitution in certain cases, like wrongful accusation in the courts ...

And the congregation sighs, 'Oh for goodness' sake! So – you've been looking it up in the books. Get on with the story.'

The second danger is importing feelings and attitudes which the text doesn't justify and yet which affect the way the story is heard. A sermon which deals with the boy Jesus in the temple and Mary and Joseph's frantic search for him must avoid making Jesus sound like a stroppy teenager. Such an interpretation could not have been in Luke's mind, is untrue to his purpose and instead of pointing us to the theology of the story, diverts us from its main point. Again, is the stable dark, dank and smelly or warm, clean and cosy? We don't actually know too much about the stable and so perhaps it would be unwise to build our main point upon the condition of the straw!

The third problem is that we get so caught up in the story that we forget that it is part of a sermon. It's possible to retell the tale but not in a way that carries a message. By this I am not advocating crudely laying the 'moral' on with a trowel. But preaching is reflecting on a text and bringing out its relevance for us today, not just doing a rather freer retelling of the biblical version. We can stay firmly in the world of the story but at some point we've got to show that there's a message for our time.

Sue Colclough manages this by putting the 'sermon' into the final prayer. She has told the story of Jesus' Nazareth sermon from the standpoint of a member of the congregation and has stayed within the world of the text. It's the prayer at the end which carries the contemporary message:

> Dear Lord Jesus, we may laugh at reactions like this
> We might wonder how people could have denied you so easily.
> But probably if we had been there in that synagogue,
> We too wouldn't have recognized you,
> We wouldn't have liked criticism about ourselves,
> We would have had preconceived ideas about the Messiah.
> We would have driven you out, and rejected you.

## THE MYTH OF THE NEUTRAL PARAPHRASE

I have spoken of the importance of allowing the imagination to be disciplined by the shape and intention of the biblical story. But of course, every retelling interprets the text from the moment it starts. There is no such thing as a neutral paraphrase. Every paraphrase carries interpretive freight. The storyteller has already made decisions about what to include or omit, what details to highlight and emphasize. The retelling has a shape, structure and movement of its own; it has its own climax. Meaning, significance and motive are built in to the narration. The emotions of the central characters are made explicit where the Bible has left them implicit. And, of course, meaning is powerfully communicated by such things as tone of voice, pauses, gestures and facial expression.

This is inevitable but I do not think it is normally a problem. Why is the preacher retelling the story if not to bring out something which is obscure or left unarticulated in the Bible story? Look at this retelling by Alison Peacock. She has opted to stay in the ancient story. There are no moves into our world. But all the time she has got her own take on the encounter of Jesus and the Syro Phoenician woman. She shows this by the way she depicts the reactions of one of the disciples:

> Despite the dust on her clothing, she looked strangely respectable and not the kind to beg at the side of the road. The woman spoke directly to the rabbi. The disciple cannot remember exactly what she said. Yet, as she spoke, he began to realize what this woman wanted. He hadn't really listened before, conscious only of noise and not words. She didn't want money, or a charm against evil. She actually wanted the rabbi himself. She wanted to drain him with her need as others had in Galilee. But this woman could have no claim on the rabbi.[1]

The theology of the sermon dominates the way the story is retold. There is nothing about the woman looking respectable in the text nor about wanting to drain Jesus with her need, but both points are legitimate. The sermonic point is carried by the phrase 'But this woman could have no claim on the rabbi' and this is the aspect which will be explored as the title 'Crossing the border' implies.

---

**EXERCISE**

*It might be helpful to analyse part of a sermon by Barbara Brown Taylor which also stays within the world of the story, though there are one or two small steps into our time. She is expounding the story of the man born blind. What techniques is she using, and to make what points?*

---

When he says that, everyone in the room stops breathing. A nobody from nowhere who was blind until about 45 minutes ago has just told the board of elders that they could not see God if God bit them on the nose. They do not let the insult go unreturned either. They rise to their full height in front of him, look down their unbitten noses into his furious new eyes, and say, 'You were born entirely in sins and are you trying to teach us?' And they drive him out.[2]

Your analysis might have picked up the following features. The preacher has worked on showing us what was happening in the room rather than just telling us. 'Everyone in the room stops breathing; rises to their full height; look down their unbitten noses; furious new eyes' – there's a dramatic dimension here. Something of the significance of the story is brought out in the phrase 'new eyes' – it is not likely that this phrase is just a comment about optics. It's about insight and revelation as well as 20/20 vision. The man sees reality differently. 'Unbitten noses' reinforces this. Their noses are unbitten because, picking up the earlier comment, God has not encountered them. There are also two forays into our world – in the colloquialisms: 'nobody from nowhere'; 'if God bit them on the nose', and the anachronistic 'board of elders'.

Retelling the story is not a way of improving on the Bible, nor smuggling in opinions which are inimical to what the Bible is trying to say. It is a way of preaching. It aims to help the congregation enter the Bible story and hear it afresh and see truths in it which it might easily have missed. Its structure is parasitic on the original but is ultimately determined by the preacher's purposes. It tries to let the Bible story be our contemporary by sharpening up similarities between its world and ours. And this will include any technique which helps it speak personally to those who hear. I want now to illustrate these different aims.


NARRATIVE FOCUS

Bible stories have a shape, and so inevitably has the preacher's paraphrase. Normally the shapes of the two versions will be roughly the same, but this does not always have to be the case. The paraphrase is sermon disguised as a retelling. Therefore its structure will serve the intention of the preacher as well as recount the original story. Henry Mitchell observes that black preachers ask themselves questions about their behavioural purpose: 'What do I want this sermon to do and therefore what shape is best?' The 'narrative focus' is in the hand of the preacher. Mitchell imagines a preacher designing a sermon on the Prodigal Son and asks, 'What is the question which will maintain suspense?' The choice is in the preacher's hands. If the sermon is about repentance then the question on which the sermon will turn will be, 'Will the boy go home?' That question will shape the sermon. If, on the other hand, the sermon is about grace then the key question will be, 'Will the father receive him?' The narrative focus always gets the emphasis, everything in the story leads up to it and it will be developed in living detail.[3]

## ANACHRONISMS

A very powerful method of letting the Bible story speak with a contemporary voice is to introduce anachronistic detail. Here is part of a sermon on the importunate widow:

> She's been going to the courthouse to do something like a Middle Eastern sit-in. She parks herself outside the judge's office door, or sits in the back of his courtroom, and buttonholes him every time he leaves. That judge can't go into his office, or out for lunch, without running into her. She probably whines 'Give me justice' 20 times a week. Maybe she makes friends with the judge's mother and his wife, hoping that they will help her to turn his heart. Finally he listens, as the Greek says, 'so she won't give me a black eye'.[4]

What is going on here? Reframing the Bible story means that we see the situation through the lens of our experience. 'They' become us. But there is leakage both ways. It is true that the biblical story is seen through the lens of our experience and we see the widow and the judge and Jesus as one of us, living in our town today. But it also works the other way round. The biblical world interprets our world and comments upon it. And because the biblical story always carries more authority, it decides who's good and who's bad, who's right and who's wrong. If you retell the parable of the Good Samaritan and make the priest and the Levite into the bishop and the churchwarden, you are not only giving the parable a contemporizing twist, you are also making negative comments about bishops and churchwardens.

When it works, this technique means that a formal application of the message isn't necessary. The message comes grafted in. Here is a sermon on the call of Moses.

> If you don't want to meet God, keep walking. Stride ahead, don't look out of the corner of your eye, ignore strange and unusual features of the landscape. Keep your curiosity on the lead. Be warned by Moses. He began the day normally enough: 'Here in my hand I have a "To do" list. And it says: 1. Look after Jethro's sheep; 2. Lead them to the far side of the desert; 3. Get to Horeb by coffee time. The mistake was turning aside. Deviating from the plan I'd mapped out for myself. I never did get the rest of the day sorted out. I suppose the sheep managed somehow. I should have gripped my copy of *The Shepherd's Gazette* firmly and kept walking. Then the day would have been like all the other days – dull, predictable, but safe and satisfying enough in its own way. The essential thing is to keep walking. Don't give him an inch or he'll take your life.'
> But if you do turn aside and enter the circle cast by the burning bush, you will meet God.

The story is reframed so as to put the listener in the footsteps of Moses, to suggest the terror and the attraction of meeting God, his ability to come into our safe routines and make disturbing demands of us.

Anachronisms can change the whole tone of a story, making it darker or more amusing than the original. A sermon on the Tribute Money moves us into the world of knockabout comedy:

> So in they came, all obsequious with wet palms and limp hand-shakes. 'Master,' they said (nice one that; wrong-foot him; make him think we're on his side), 'Master, we know you're an honest and learned man who would have had an Oxford degree if you'd been living somewhat later. And we know you're not afraid of anyone, not nasty Mr Pilate from Rome, and certainly not a group of slimy toads like us. So tell us: should we pay taxes to Caesar or not? I mean, we don't want to bother you, but we've just got this self-assessment form and before we go to all this trouble we'd like to know what you think.' That should do it, they thought. Nicely trapped. If he says, 'Of course you should pay it', he'll be drummed

out of the Brownies by every self-respecting nationalist in
Jerusalem; if on the other hand he says 'Don't pay', he'll be walking
straight into a charge of treason. 15-love.[5]

You might want to pause for a moment to ask yourself what the effect of
this retelling is. Does it trivialize the original? Or does it helpfully play up
the battle of wits between Jesus and his opponents? All sermon decisions
involve a cost–benefit calculation. Do the advantages of John Pritchard's
approach outweigh the disadvantages, and how would you express both? If
you were paraphrasing the incident, how would you use anachronistic
detail?

Go back to the extract with which this chapter began. This is chock full
of anachronisms. In fact it may be hard to spot the points at which the
sermon touches the original story in the New Testament. To be fair to the
preacher, the sermon does come home to rest eventually. So what is he or
she trying to do here? I would suggest the sermon is trying to establish
early on that the people to whom Jesus came (via the baptism of John)
were not much different from the people of our day. This allows the
preacher to emphasize that the Jesus who stood in the water with them,
identifying with them in their lostness and their longing, is the same Jesus
who stands with us. And that is the rationale for using anachronisms.

## COMMUNICATING THE FORCE

We have already seen that retelling the brief Bible story will require the
preacher to expand some details and supply, even invent, others. I've suggested that the process should recognize the control of the original but
accept that often the result will appear to have been over-free. Whether a
retelling is justified or not depends, I think, primarily on how far it communicates the force and significance of the original story. Here is an
extreme example which I think works admirably. It comes from a sermon
by a black preacher on Peter's walking on the water.

But just in the height of the fear, Jesus said, 'Stop being afraid . . .
It is I.' And this daring man, with reckless faith, said 'Lord, if it be
thou, suffer me to come to you walking on the water.' He said,
'Come on.' So Simon started to leave the boat and the other men

59

laid a restraining hand on him and said, 'Don't be stupid . . . be practical . . . You've been about lakes all your life. Haven't you had enough?' But he said, 'Jesus told me to come.' But he said, 'Listen, we all love him and we all know he has great power, but that's water, Simon, and no man has ever walked on water!' But he said, 'That's the Lord.' He said, 'I know it's the Lord but be practical.' But Simon said, 'When the Lord calls, sometimes you lose the sense of what is practical, and right now my faith has become reckless and daring and I'm going.' And the records said, 'He walked on water!' Oh, I know, I know you're going to say, 'But he sank.' But he walked! He walked on the water! And when he started from the boat, the laws of nature said, 'Here comes a man walking, Lord, on the water; and you know that this is against the laws of gravitation; what shall we do?' He said, 'With faith like this, you might suspend the natural laws, because we all have to meet a faith like this with an unusual suspension of the law. And if he has faith to walk . . . let him walk!'[6]

You will search in vain for the conversation between the laws of nature and God, but I think this rendering brings out the force and significance of Matthew's account.

## COME AND SEE FOR YOURSELF

The final set of examples focuses on those retellings which try to bring the listener into the story in his or her own person. We are familiar with first-person 'stream of consciousness' type sermons; the congregation eaves-drops on one of the characters. It's a well-tried technique. This strategy is different. The listener is invited to be present in the story. The first example comes from a sermon on Jesus washing the disciples' feet:

There is no sound except the sound of water running down into the basin. And then the almost imperceptible sound of a towel drying the skin. You can hear Jesus move to the next person. No one speaks. The silence is excruciating. Why doesn't somebody say something? You know very well. This is an uncomfortable moment. No one knows where to look. The disciple whose feet are being washed cannot bring himself to meet Jesus' gaze. Just the sound of water running into a basin.

So look away. Your eye catches sight of the outer garment crumpled in the corner. He laid that by. Along with everything else – glory, status and the life of heaven. You stare fixedly at the edge of the towel. That symbol of everything he took on – a life of humility and service, the form of a slave, obedience unto death, human flesh. And he is coming nearer and nearer to you. Soon it will be you who will feel his hands and hear the water running down. And be acutely aware of the fact that he is kneeling at your feet while you remain seated. Will no one break the silence? Thank God he gets to Peter before he gets to you. And Peter bursts out in protest, voicing what everyone else feels: You shall never wash my feet.

It would be easy to retell that story from the point of view of one of the disciples – a variant on the 'My name is Daniel ben Joseph and I have a small farm in Galilee.' In fact, it's told from a third-person standpoint. What makes it personal is that the narrator sees each listener in the congregation as present in the upper room experiencing the foot-washing for him or herself. But the preacher retains the narrator's ability to know and express the inner thoughts and feelings of the characters.

Finally, I offer a retelling of Peter's walking on the water by Kathy Galloway of the Iona Community. It has kept very little of the original story but still manages to put the congregation in the shoes of Peter. Is this a retelling in the sense in which I've been using it? I'm not sure. But, however free ranging, it remains a very powerful sermon on the passage.

Voice 1   Come!
Voice 2   I can't do it.
Voice 1   You can do it.
Voice 2   I'm too heavy. I'll sink.
Voice 1   Lay down your burdens and you'll be light enough.
Voice 2   I'm not strong enough.
Voice 1   You don't have to be strong. The water will hold you up.
Voice 2   I might get wet.
Voice 1   Yes, you will.
Voice 2   I might sink.

| Voice 1 | Only if you panic. |
|---------|--------------------|
| Voice 2 | I might drown. |
| Voice 1 | You won't drown. Just let yourself float, and the water will carry you. |
| Voice 2 | People will see me. |
| Voice 1 | Yes, they'll definitely see you. You might encourage some of them to try it too. |
| Voice 2 | But some of them might try to stop me, for my own good. |
| Voice 1 | Yes. But you can't live out of other people's fears. |
| Voice 2 | Some of them might throw stones at me. |
| Voice 1 | That's a risk you'll just have to take. |
| Voice 2 | Some of them might laugh at me. |
| Voice 1 | Yes. But you'll be the one walking on the water. |
| Voice 2 | The water's very dark. |
| Voice 1 | That's just because you're standing in the shadow. From here, it's a beautiful green. |
| Voice 2 | There might be monsters. |
| Voice 1 | Yes. But there are monsters where you are now. |
| Voice 2 | How will I know which direction to walk in? |
| Voice 1 | Just keep your eyes on me. |
| Voice 2 | What if I can't see you for the waves? |
| Voice 1 | I'll still be here. |
| Voice 2 | I'm very scared. |
| Voice 1 | We're all scared. But don't trust your fears. They're not reliable. |
| Voice 2 | What will I trust? |
| Voice 1 | Trust your love. |
| Voice 2 | But what if I get that wrong? |
| Voice 1 | Then trust my love. They come from the same place. |
| Voice 2 | But what if . . . ? |
| Voice 1 | This conversation's becoming very circular. I'm not going to stand here all day while you theorize. Now you have to move your body. Action will remove the doubt. Are you coming?[7] |

# 7 Telling it slant

*Images, analogies and metaphors*

Feeling in the need of stimulation, I turned the television on to watch a documentary on how the brain works. The presenter was making a point about the way in which input from outside makes tracks in the brain. At considerable expense we were taken to South America to watch him standing on one side of a gorge showing how a bridge had to be thrown from one side to the other in order to connect the two sides and allow traffic between them. This was similar to what is happening all the time in the brain, he explained. Or, to put it another way . . . and suddenly we were watching two children running around in a cornfield trampling the corn as they chased each other and leaving circles in the crop. I remember feeling slightly irritated that we viewers were thought to need two images before we could grasp what was a fairly basic idea. But, maddeningly, the image of the children stayed with me for the rest of the week and, as you can see, for the next nine months at least.

Preaching that embodies the Word also makes heavy use of images, pictures, analogies, similes and metaphors. It's possible to make fine distinctions between these terms but it's not vital to do so for the moment. What we do need to appreciate is that embodying an idea in a carefully chosen image or analogy is one of the best ways of explaining it. The great doctrines of Christianity began life as pictures: redemption, justification, election, repentance – bought out of slavery, pronounced not guilty, picked out of the crowd, changing your outlook.

The popularizers of science know this well. Light is like billiard balls cannoning into one another or like the wind passing over a field of wheat. Space is like a rubber sheet being stretched in all directions. Listen to Bill Bryson explaining why the chances of a 1,055 sequence molecule like collagen spontaneously self-assembling are nil.

> To grasp what a long shot its existence is, visualize a standard Las Vegas slot machine but broadened greatly – to about 27 metres, to

be precise – to accompany 1,055 spinning wheels instead of the usual three or four and with twenty symbols on each wheel (one for each amino acid). How long would you have to pull the handle before all 1,055 symbols came up in the right order? Effectively, for ever.[1]

Images, analogies, visual pictures of one kind or another are central to the sermon's task of communicating ideas. It makes a big difference if the preacher depicts God as a grumpy old man viewing the world at a distance through binoculars or as a cosmic waiter rushing about trying to satisfy our every whim. Both images are active in the popular theologies of our society. The task for the preacher who wants to offer a different concept of God is to find a satisfying image that will do the job.

A successful analogy or image finds a point of contact between its world and the world of the referent. Sometimes it works by reframing the subject so that we see it in a new perspective. Or it behaves like a filter and colours the idea. For this reason, some writers prefer to call them 'onlooks', because they invite people to 'look on X as if it were Y'. For example, I once asked an archdeacon what his job was. He might have been clever-clever and given the famous answer: 'An archdeacon is an ecclesiastical dignitary who performs archidiaconal functions.' What he actually said was: 'Look at it this way. I'm the bishop's rottweiler.' Then at last I understood.

---

**EXERCISE**

*It is worth looking over a recent sermon and counting the number of images, analogies or word pictures which it contains. Very often a sermon is dull because it lacks word pictures. It's the images which tweak the imagination and force us to look at old truths in a new way.*

*And here's an image looking for a sermon: focusing the sun's rays with a magnifying glass until you produce a single, tiny, white-hot point of light. How would you use this word picture?*

---

There are a number of possibilities. Perhaps it will illustrate the Bible's capacity suddenly and painfully to speak to us and make our hearts burn. Or will it do a better job as a way of representing the idea of the Divine nature and glory sharply focused in Jesus?

## REORDERING THE MIND

Images have enormous power. In fact the best communicators have always made extensive use of pictures, models and metaphors. Eva Kittay said that 'metaphors re-arrange the furniture of the mind'.[2] C. S. Lewis would sometimes link three or four images or analogies together in a kind of all-out assault on the imagination.[3] Images help us understand with our senses; we see, hear and feel the message. Barbara Brown Taylor reminds us: 'We must not assume that the important work of faith takes place in the bright-lit arenas of explanation and action instead of further down the scale, in the life-like shadows of experience and image.'[4] Unfortunately, over the years, Christian communication has tended to drift away from pictures towards propositions, with the result that sermons often sound more like explanations than invitations to let the imagination play.

Presumably it's because images assault the senses that they stay in the memory, like the children in the cornfield. We know the experience of looking at an object against a source of light, in front of a window or a light bulb. When you close your eyes the after-image remains (even though reversed). A powerful image in a sermon can imprint itself on consciousness, returning to the mind again and again in the days that follow.

Some examples may help illustrate this claim:

- In his enthronement sermon Archbishop Rowan Williams used the image of God as a conservationist in an art gallery patiently working away at a picture to remove the grime, the oil and the dust, in order to reveal, lay bare, 'to let us appear in our true colours'.
- A sermon on the apostle Thomas describes him as reading the palms of Jesus like Braille because, at that point in the story, Thomas is blind.
- From an Advent sermon: 'I have a friend who visited Moscow and saw people joining queues when they had no idea where the queue was leading. But they queued in the faith that there would be something worth having at the end. Advent is like that, standing in God's queue,

hanging about, waiting . . . with something worth waiting for at the end.'[5]

- In a throwaway comment a preacher describes the Bible as 'God's pop-up book'.
- Here's an image of the Church as pieces on a chess board: 'Sometimes it can look as if the Church is in the latter stages of the game, where the bishops are moving diagonally – and somewhat eccentrically – across the board; the knights – who chair the committees – are taking one step forwards and two steps sideways; the safe castles have all been taken (with freehold); the pawns are being moved around as necessary; and the King himself seems to be trapped and unable to move. How long, they say, before it's check-mate?'[6]
- And an extended analogy from a sermon on Luke 21: 'The signs of the end are only what we would expect. When good erupts into our world evil reacts badly. These are the death convulsions of the Beast, the roar of wounded Evil. The conflict in the cosmos is mirrored on earth. The Kingdom of Satan has been dealt a fatal blow and it writhes in its death throes. Like a wounded animal, it spits and snarls. Evil gives up its prey slowly, reluctantly. Its dead man's grip has to be broken, joint by joint. But Christ is Lord and the cross and resurrection are the mark of his triumph.'

---

**EXERCISE**

*You are preaching on 'Seek first the kingdom of God' and you need an analogy for the main idea. You have already decided that this means being single-minded, absorbed in only one thing, totally concentrated on the matter in hand. What word pictures come to mind?*

---

This is the way one preacher tackled the task:

Take the rifle-shooting in the Olympics. Watch any competitor and you will see a picture of total concentration. Everything is focused down the barrel of the gun on to the target – eye, hand, finger, arms, stance. Apparently Olympics competitors can control the breathing so that they lower the heart rate. But what does he *not* notice? The pressure of his clothes; the sound of spectators talking quietly; a loudspeaker announcement far away; the need to get the car serviced; what he will eat for dinner tonight; the TV programme he has videoed; his need for a haircut. These things don't go away but they get pushed to the side by the power of the one thing he's got his eyes fixed on. So seek first the kingdom of God.

## WHEN IMAGES FAIL

Images don't always work, however, and it's worth trying to discover why.

First, some images are just too unpleasant for the listeners to take. A Christmas message contained the image of the incarnation as 'God injecting himself into the world's blood stream'. It was a vivid picture, certainly, but a number of people found the motif of the hypodermic needle and the hospital context too painful to dwell on.

Second, some images don't work because they divert attention from the point of the sermon. I still enjoy the memory of a good friend of mine describing Jesus as a light. Christ's attractiveness meant that people were drawn to him. 'Just like the candle flame to which all the moths are . . .' (drawn so that they die in agony, presumably). Just in time he saw that this image really wasn't quite doing the job he hoped for and had the confidence to turn it into a joke with the congregation.

Third, some analogies trivialize what is holy. For example, God is not much like a duvet nor Jesus like Coca-Cola.

Fourth, some word pictures tend towards the sentimental. I'm fond of the image in the old hymn: 'In our dear Lord's garden, planted here below, many tiny flowerets in sweet beauty grow.' I know this to be true because I've seen them, fighting to get on to the school bus, with mobiles clasped to their ears, flowerets every one.

Fifth, many images fail to have the impact they once had because they have become humdrum and threadbare. Word pictures which once excited and delighted us can go stale. Have you heard any of these phrases before?

So, when the cookie crumbles and the rubber hits the road, we need to draw a line under this and move on. Let's touch base soon and apply some blue-sky thinking to the problem. I mean, we may be between a rock and a hard place but it's not rocket science. Anyway, thanks for your input. I'd like to park it for now and unwrap it later. And the bottom line is, I am, like, so outta here.

Sermons are not immune from stale images. Stephen Wright, director of the College of Preachers, writes about Cliché Corner and examines the stock phrase 'On our television screens'. He remarks that once upon a time this

> was an attempt to be vivid, to evoke a sense of the picture being actually beamed into our living rooms. Now it's a tell-tale sign of a standardized piece of backcloth in a sermon. It does nothing to bring home to people the reality of terrible things. It reinforces the feeling that this preacher has little of interest to say – a simplistic tirade against an evil world or an equally simplistic invitation to pietist escapism.[7]

Many images which make frequent appearances in sermons have become threadbare. We have to work at an idea like 'Jesus became a human being just like us. He took on flesh and blood' because it has ceased to shock us. Perhaps it's time to take a break from Holman Hunt's 'Light of the World', because so many preachers have described the portrait of Christ at the door of humanity's heart, and have made much of the fact that the door has no handle 'because the handle is on the inside'. Sermons on temptation return to the picture: 'You can't stop birds flying over your head but you can stop them making nests in your hair.' There was a time when no sermon was complete without a reference to the Velveteen rabbit. Now it's as likely to be a paraphrase of the poem 'Foot-prints'. Recently I seem to have heard over and over again a story about a boy throwing starfish back into the sea with the punch line 'It mattered to him.' These images make an impact when they are heard for the first time, but the preacher has to be careful not to do them to death. Perhaps after a suitable rest even the Velveteen Rabbit can hop into life again.

You might begin by asking what the word 'abide' implies in its context. At its most basic it means 'staying in the same place' (literally 'remain'). But it carries the extra sense of staying connected. Horticultural images may not be the best ones since Jesus has already given us the picture of the vine and its branches. What else can you come up with?

Groups which have tried this exercise have produced a large number of suggestions, of which I list a few:

- resting in an armchair;
- pitching your tent for the night;
- holding hands with someone you love;
- a branch of an apple tree; a skin graft;
- the *Mr and Mrs Game Show* (essentially knowing someone so well that you almost inhabit their personality);
- being connected by a blood transfusion;
- being a child in the womb;
- using a mobile phone;
- having a bleep (with the possibility of turning it off so that you cannot be contacted);
- talking a plane down (emphasizing obedience to instructions);
- having your computer taken over by remote control;
- learning to drive (knowing that the driving instructor has her own set of controls and could drive you round the roundabout without your involvement);
- a mother telling her child, 'Stay there and don't wander off';

- an orchestra in touch with the conductor;
- a choir;
- line-dancing;
- the contacts of the TV remote control getting dirty and being unable to switch channels;
- two people pretending to be one person seeing his or her reflection and mirroring their actions exactly;
- a couple ballroom dancing.

The advantage of a long list is that you can afford to be picky. Some of these are too mechanical and automatic – Jesus is speaking of a personal relationship, not just plugging in to a power socket. Some are too passive – we are actively involved or Jesus wouldn't command us to abide. But one of the others may do, especially if it suggests keeping in touch and not allowing the link to be broken. If it were your sermon, which would you choose? Or did you come up with one that's better than any of those above?

## WHEN THE MIND GOES BLANK

The preceding exercise may have highlighted a problem. Some people find it extremely difficult to think of images. Try as they might, nothing comes. Given the crucial importance of making preaching visual, are there any strategies which can help? I want to suggest two.

### Expand the image which is already in the biblical Word

Very often the Bible passage you are working with will contain images in embryo. One method for kickstarting the imagination is to work with these. Commentaries are fond of pointing out that this or that Greek word is literally such and such or that at its heart is the picture of so and so. Mull over these images, play free association with them, imagine what they might look like if you saw or heard them, ransack the lexicon to see how these words are used in non-technical contexts. This is not so that you can say, 'Well the Greek word *dunamis* gives us our word "dynamite"' – the power of the Holy Spirit isn't much like dynamite – it's to help you generate a live image for the sermon.

As an example, we might look at two images in James. 'Faith by itself, if it has no works, is dead' (2.17) and 'You believe that God is one; you do well. Even the demons believe – and shudder' (2.19). How might these be mined for a sermon?

The first refers to a body on the slab, laid out in the morgue. It is easily identified by the next of kin. Strangely, in its appearance it looks healthier than it did when it was still alive. In every respect it is exactly like the person who was known and loved by friends but . . . it is different; it has no life in it. And soon it will decay and putrefy. As the body without the spirit is dead, so faith without deeds is dead.

The other verse is a dark parody of the creed. 'Do you believe in God?' James asks. 'Yes,' says the congregation. 'Do you believe in God?' he asks the hosts of hell, and the demons reply 'Yes', even though their voices quaver as they say it. Demons don't have doubts about the existence of God nor do they have crises of faith. In fact they almost certainly believe more firmly and unshakably than the average Christian. But what is their belief worth? 'Nothing,' says James, 'without a life which matches that profession.'

Preparing to preach on forgiveness, you look up the word to 'forgive'. The dictionary tells you that literally the Greek verb means 'to let go'. It offers examples: a king lets a debt go. Jesus lets out a loud cry – and lets his spirit go. The word is used of letting a wife go in divorce, and of abandoning a house, of leaving your nets behind you, and, interestingly, of walking away from a fire and letting it burn itself out. Now you may have a way in to the sermon. Forgiveness can be presented as letting it go.

Let go of what, exactly? Let go of the hatred. And of the desire for revenge. Let go of the refusal to help the person if they were in desperate need. And let go of the resentment which rises up as you think of the offence. Etymologically, re-sentment is to feel something all over again. So stop rerunning the video of the incident. Stop freeze-framing it, feeling all over again the slight, the hurt, the insult, the pain. Let it go.

## Make forced connections

There's an ancient parlour game called the 'The Coffee Pot Game'. It relies on making forced connections. Players have to say in what way a particular object or person is like a coffee pot. The game is only for fun, of course, and is very artificial. It may sound like creative thinking by numbers. If you have played it, however, you are surprised at how being compelled to make connections generates examples you would never have thought of otherwise.

Wayne McDill has formalized the technique into a series of steps. First, he says, you need to state as clearly as possible the idea in the sermon which you are trying to illustrate. Then you express the concept in general terms, as an abstraction or a principle or a proposition. The third step is to write down as many non-religious areas of life as you wish – home, family, relationships, sport, work, the natural world, animals, politics, entertainment, film, etc. Then work systematically through these areas, trying to think of examples of the generalized concept. The final stage is to make these examples as specific as possible. Translate them downwards into concrete stories, particular instances, vivid pictures.[8]

This may seem a laboured process, so an example may help. You want to illustrate the idea that *in Christ God was reconciling the world to himself.* The generalized idea might be that someone can use another person as his or her agent and work through them. You look for examples of this abstract principle in non-religious areas of life – in the home, your physical body, the world of sport, of business, politics, etc. You pull out examples of company representatives, agents, those acting on behalf of an institution, ministry spokespersons, go-betweens, ambassadors, soldiers acting under commanding officers, children running errands, builders putting architects' plans into execution and so on. Then you try to turn each abstract example into a highly specific image or picture.

At the end of the process, this is what one preacher came up with:

In Christ we see God at work. From time to time I have to clear out the drain at the front of the house. I lift the drain cover, wrinkle my nose and put my hand deep down into the muck, decaying leaves, slime, all the unspeakable gunge that accumulates and blocks the drain. Now don't waste time saying, 'Oh your poor hand! How could you possibly force it to do that, how could you inflict such indignity on your hand?' The hand and I are the same person. What I do, my hand does. What my hand does, I do. And what God does, Jesus does. And what Jesus does, God does. Through Jesus, God begins the process of getting through to us and cleaning us up. So Jesus is called the beginning. And when God starts all over again, he gets his hands dirty.

When we turn towards images and word pictures, we are recognizing that Jesus did not say something like 'Wealth is a grave hindrance to true religion.' He said, 'It is easier for a camel to go through the eye of a needle than for a rich man to enter the kingdom of heaven.'

# 8  A slice of life

*Instances and examples*

The previous chapter dealt with images, metaphors, similes and analogies, but they are not the only way of embodying an idea. Very often what we need are not more analogies or metaphors but actual examples of the concept we are dealing with. We need a slice of real life. If images say, 'It is something like this' or 'See this idea through the filter of this picture', then instances say, 'This is a tiny example of what I mean.' Not 'It is like this' but 'It *is* this.'

A sermon on Lazarus by Jolyon Mitchell illustrates the distinction. He begins, 'The story in John takes us into such grief and loss' and follows this remark with an image. 'And we're met. Met not by a God who folds his arms, and puts on a serene and distant smile; rather by a God who has made himself vulnerable, a God who has experienced grief, anger and loss.'

The God of the serene and distant smile makes for a telling image, but the whole paragraph is preceded by an instance, a real example of grief and loss:

> I vividly remember standing at a friend's funeral. Watching as they lowered the coffin in. Just 18 and tragically killed in a car crash. Two others had died. It wasn't their fault either. I found myself wondering 'Why?' and 'Why them, God?' And there was no answer but the windy rain, the smart black shoes squelching in the mud, and parents holding each other as they sobbed.[1]

Instances are glimpses of what we are talking about. They are film-like in the way they capture a mental picture of a scene. They freeze-frame a real example of the abstract idea. They are particular and specific.

The following excerpt shows how a group of instances, each of which is briefly drawn, can shed light on an idea from different angles. This is one of the commonest and most effective uses of instances, preaching them on the hoof, spraying them in twos or threes. In this example, the preacher is exploring the difference it makes to know that your life has been saved by someone else.

> A man plunges into a river to save a drowning child, but in doing so loses his own life. Someone tries to overpower a crazed gunman in a shooting spree in a McDonalds, and dies in the process, but saves others. A fireman pulls a child from a burning building, but is himself consumed by the flames. Such things are rare but they happen. What a difference it must make to me, if my life has been saved by another![2]

## SPILLING BLOOD AND DRAWING TEETH

Thinking of instances is hard work. It is my impression that on the whole preachers are pretty good at using images but exploit the power of instances less frequently. It's easy to feel, 'For Heaven's sake! I've spent hours on this sermon. I've worked at the exegesis and the exposition. I've honed this abstract distillation of the message. Don't I get a break? What's the point of fleshing out what is perfectly clear? Especially when it is going to hurt my brain to do it.'

It would be useful to take your last half-dozen sermons and count the number of instances you used. How many were there per sermon? What would be the effect of removing them? And what would have happened to the sermon if you had filled out your bare points with yet more instances?

---

**EXERCISE**

*Here are some 'bare points' about prayer. 'Prayer is difficult', 'Our thoughts wander', 'It is sometimes hard to stay focused on God.' Try to fill them out with actual examples of what it is like to pray and find your thoughts wandering. Think of what it would be like to have your prayers recorded and played back in public? The wandering thoughts, the inability to stay focused on God – it would be a nightmare.*

---

Here's one possibility:

> Hello, God. Here I am again. This coffee's not special and we're
> nearly out of milk. I want to thank you for answering my prayers –
> Mrs Snodgrass was much better yesterday when I called. Is that the
> newspaper coming through the door? Wonder how United got on?
> Forgive me the uncharitable thoughts I had about my boss. I can
> see dust on top of the television. I wonder what's on tonight? Oh no,
> we're going out tonight. Whoops, sorry Lord. I drifted off. Where
> was I? Oh yes, the floods in West Sussex.

The high-level generalizing comment leaves the listeners detached. There
is a real chance that they won't engage with the concept if it isn't given
shape, colour and movement through an actual instance. The specific
example carries enormous communicative power and energy.

As an illustration of this, listen to the beginning of a sermon on Mary
and Martha (Luke 10.38–42) by Martha Anderson:

> And I said, 'I am worried and distracted about many things. I am
> worried and distracted by environmental destruction, by war and
> drought and poverty and disease and racism. I am worried about an
> 88-year-old woman from my last parish whose heart is failing. I am
> worried about my daughter who works too hard and is always tired.
> I am worried about all the folks who are listening to me today,
> coping with all they have been through in the last year and a half. I
> am worried about finding enough money to pay the mortgage each
> month, about whether the car is parked legally, about how to find
> time to get my hair cut. And today', I say to Jesus, 'I am especially
> worried and distracted about this story of you and me and my sister
> in Bethany. It worries me because I know what you are going to say:
> that Mary sitting at your feet and listening while I slave away in the
> kitchen, has the better part.'[3]

The particular examples of being worried and distracted lock into the congregation's suspicions that, once again, it's going to be told off for being
busy.

## 'LET ME GIVE YOU AN EXAMPLE'

Most of us actually find it quite difficult to understand what someone is saying without an example. A friend says, 'Work's terrible at the moment.' 'What do you mean?', we say, looking for a couple of instances. It isn't just a matter of holding our attention; we don't know what they mean until they flesh out the general statement. Instances are central to understanding. 'Can you give me an example?' is a standard response to any statement of a principle.

For example, a statement like 'God speaks to us in the big events of our lives' is fine as far as it goes. We might try an image, borrowing C. S. Lewis' 'God speaks in our joys but shouts in our pain.' But the idea is filled out best by listing particular instances of how God might speak through life events, as in this sermon by Catherine Byrom:

> Perhaps it was the loss of a job that started you looking for a purpose. Perhaps it was the death of someone close to you that got you asking where God was in suffering. Or about life after death. Perhaps it was a happy crisis – like the birth of a child – that just made you want to thank somebody, or to take your spiritual life more seriously for the sake of the child.

Even here she might have gone to an even deeper level of particularity: 'until they gave you twenty minutes to clear your desk and told you to leave the keys to the firm's car', 'the death of your mother in the Spring', 'the birth of little Abigail'. 'Take your spiritual life more seriously' is another phrase which could be made more specific – how might someone take their spiritual life more seriously? What might that look like? Nevertheless, the instances do their job. They answer the question: 'What do you mean? Can you give me an example?'

## SHARPENING THE FOCUS

The above example suggests that the essence of a good instance is its specific nature. To make an event or situation specific we need to visualize it, to see it as a film script. We need to take stills. Very often we go only halfway on this. For example, the sentence 'We see this kind of thing on our television screens daily' feels like a half-hearted attempt at an instance.

It's much stronger to go several levels down. What's actually on the television? 'Seven-year-old boys with guns in their hands and 14-year-old girls with the eyes of old women' might make the point more sharply. So referring to *Match of the Day* is preferable to 'football on television'. 'Chanel Number 5' beats 'expensive perfume'.

Notice the effect of the instance in this sermon on Romans 6.1–11:

> The last word on the matter is resurrection. Not 'resuscitation' as if Jesus were the victim of a road traffic accident, brought back to life with 15 litres of blood and a cardiac shock machine – only to die again sometime.

A sermon on John the Baptist exhorts us to focus on Christ and find that our priorities change. But the punch is in the instances:

> When our focus is on Christ we might find that buying a new kitchen might not seem as important as giving to a homeless hostel. Or the day at the golf club might become less appealing than taking time to repair a broken relationship.

I'm inclined to say that it is always better to go down to deeper levels of specificity than risk staying with the general comment. But, of course, it's possible to take this principle too far, as this spoof example illustrates:

> Have you ever been up a step-ladder and lost your balance and grabbed at a frayed light fitting with your bare hands and been electrocuted? I have. Oooh, it didn't half sting. And have you ever tried to lose weight by having your jaws wired together and found you were up half the night trying to liquidize peanut brittle? My neighbour has. Because life's not fair. Is it? Some of us drink champagne in the fast lane and some of us eat our sandwiches by the loose chippings on the A597.[4]

There are problems with instances, of course. Because they are by nature specific and particular they raise the question of stereotyping. Some people feel that the value of the abstract idea lies precisely in the fact that it doesn't get tangled up in controversial detail. They suggest that general statements cover the whole range of possibilities like an umbrella, just because that's what they are – high-level abstractions. Particular examples, they argue, leave three-quarters of the congregation feeling 'This has nothing to do with me.'

My impression is that the opposite is true. I think that congregations find it extremely difficult to think of how a principle or proposition applies to them without an instance. They find it much easier to do so, however, if they have an instance to work with, even if that instance is not particular to them.

Furthermore, it's important not to exaggerate the problem of typecasting. No doubt there were people in Jesus' day who said, 'I'm an elder son and I've never treated my father or younger brother in that way. We're not all miserable party poopers eaten up by jealousy, you know.' There were those who heard the parable of the Good Samaritan who retorted, 'Some of my best friends are priests and Levites. You couldn't come across a nicer bunch of people.' Any specific example runs the risk of appearing to present this particular situation as the norm.

It's as well to be aware of the dangers; but in my view, avoiding instances and sticking with abstractions is to pay too high a price. Perhaps the best we can do is to try to spread our examples across a range of life situations, involving a diversity of characters. We can try to be careful that, in one sermon or, more likely, in our preaching generally, we do not draw examples mainly from family life, or the world of work, or football or world cruises or whatever. Similarly, it will not help to depict every teenager as awkward or every woman as needy and emotional or every man as competitive and achievement-oriented. John McClure has suggested that we formalize this process, listing the life areas and sub-cultures from which illustrations are drawn, the roles played by men and women, old and young, and different ethnic groups, even checking into which centuries we dip when we want an example.[5]

I've tried this exercise with a number of groups and have found that there are some people for whom this is an incredibly difficult task. It may be possible to kick-start instances by using the technique I outlined in the previous chapter. But all of us find this hard work. This is where we spill the blood and sweat. It is easier to stay in the language of abstraction. However, I believe that it is work that has to be done if ideas, concepts, principles and doctrines are going to get off the page.

One person tackled Example 3 and worked it up into a sermon, of which this is an excerpt:

I can see the pattern written small but authentically in many people who in an honest and good heart try to follow Christ's way. I see it in a granny who said to me, 'The little lad comes to me after school for half an hour and I do his spellings with him.' I see it even in the totally banal, utterly domestic acts of service – putting out the wheelie bin, cleaning the cooker, not ignoring the fact that the cat has been sick (hoping that someone else will have cleared it up by the time we get back in the evening). I see it in a word of apology which is hard to say but unlocks a door of reconciliation. I see it in the teacher who every day took a child's soiled underwear and put clean clothes on him and took the dirty ones home to wash. And did that for weeks on end – so that the child would not be ridiculed. The pattern appears in a youth club leader who spends Tuesday nights playing with alienated teenagers, when she could be doing something else. In a friend who spends time listening to someone who is depressed, finding it a draining and exhausting business but not giving up. I see it in the couple who say to the harassed single mother, 'We'll have the kids for the weekend' and in the person who sits at three in the morning with a friend who's got a drink problem, just sitting but taking a fair amount of abuse in the process.

There are probably too many examples here. The congregation would find it hard to keep pace and would end up feeling exhausted. Also, I suspect that the instance of the teacher is too unusual and too striking not to be distracting. In fact, it's a prime example of an instance which is crying out to become a story; we want to hear it developed. But the piece beautifully demonstrates the value of instances in putting flesh on an idea.

I end this chapter with one more example. It is based on Matthew 9.36: 'When he saw the crowds, he had compassion for them.' It would have been easy to speak in general terms about Jesus' compassion and care. The preacher takes a different tack and opts for a string of instances:

Sometimes people are a pain. They get in front of me in the queue in the post office. They cut me up at roundabouts. They come up on the outside when two lanes go into one. And as they cut in they wave cheerily as if I had encouraged them to do it. They lie on television and say they haven't had affairs when everyone knows they have. They get drunk and leave the remains of curry on the pavement. They talk loudly on their mobiles on trains – very loudly so that no one can concentrate. They earn more money than is good for them playing football and then go off and marry Spice Girls. They spend thousands on the Lottery. They watch porn on the

Internet. They play their music too loud. They let their dogs mess in the park.

People are a pain.

When Jesus saw the crowds, he had compassion for them, because they were harassed and helpless, like sheep without a shepherd.

# 9  Where the saints have trod

*Testimonies and holy history*

Most instances work like photographic stills. They take an idea and give us a very brief example of what it might look like in real life. But sometimes we want to expand the one-liner. We feel that we need a little story. *Testimonies* or *accounts* are attempts to put a face on ideas by embodying them in the lives of people. We see what a concept means and what it entails by hearing how it was expressed in someone's actions. Strictly speaking, testimonies would refer to somebody's story expressed in the first person, while accounts consist of the story told by someone else. Both aim to embody the vision of Christ and its expression in daily life through someone's faith-story.

There is no shortage of examples within the Christian tradition. Hagiography, or writing improving biographies of the saints, has been a thriving industry in the history of the Church. The tone of the conventional Life of the saint is pretty much like this spoof holy history of St Confitura of Warsaw, known affectionately as Roly Poly because of her habit of rolling along the ground when in a mystical trance:

> St Confitura of Warsaw entered the convent of the Sisters of Perpetual Umbrage as a young novice and rose steadily through the ranks of pique minor and pique major until she became Greatly Miffed at the age of 27. The better manuscripts often refer to her as Rotunda because of her ample girth and her habit of eating small capsules of nitro glycerine. When annoyed, she was likely to blow up out of all proportion. She ate large quantities of garlic to keep the forces of evil away with the result that towards the end of her life she had few, if any, companions. In her last illness the sisters came and covered her with lard and she went downhill very quickly after that.[1]

## TRANSPARENT MEMBRANE

Thomas Hefferson, a specialist in hagiography, makes an important point about the way holy history works. He says that the subject of the story is 'a type of transparent membrane through which the author is intent to show the continual passage of God's grace'.[2] The biographical excerpt is designed to show what the grace of God looks like when it shines through a particular person.

Once you turn to Church history, the resources available to the preacher are vast. It is easy to find information on St Francis, Teresa of Avila, and Bernadette. Potted biographies supply all you want on Martin Luther, Lord Shaftsbury, and William Wilberforce. Some great Christians regularly appear in the charts – Cuthbert, Aidan and Patrick, Elizabeth Fry, William Booth, Mother Teresa, Martin Luther King, David Watson, John Wimber – the list is endless. Each one illustrates some aspect of the glory of Christ shining through the transparent membrane of this life.

## THE BURDEN OF HOLY HISTORY

It seems almost churlish to carp at the wealth of material. But I do want to raise questions about too easily using stories drawn from the lives of great men and women of faith. In the first place, there is a burden of holy history. Most of these characters are too good. Those listening to the sermon (never mind the preacher) feel that such godliness is beyond them. Charles Simeon rises at four in the morning, lays and lights his fire and then prays for about four hours. John Wesley rides, prays and preaches every hour God gives. George Müller lives such a life of radical faith that he is often trusting God for bread even as the children at his orphanage sit down to breakfast with nothing on the table. (But the bread arrives because a baker feels that he 'must bake bread for Müller's children'.) Confronted with such stories I feel like the psalmist: 'It is too high. I cannot attain unto it.' It really doesn't help to know that by the time I've got the car out of the garage Wesley would have ridden 20 miles and preached three sermons.

Second, these stories often make Christianity seem weird. Holy histories reflect their historical context and exemplify what was considered a virtue in the Church of the time. A fascinating article by Jane Speck focuses on the lives of Joane of the Cross and Maria Magdalene de' Pazzi. Both saints inflicted terrible pain on themselves in an attempt to share part of Christ's suffering and atone in some way for their own unworthiness. Speck probes beneath the surface of their behaviour and uncovers self-loathing and a hatred of the body (and, paradoxically, a degree of self-empowerment).[3] The implication of this is that the contemporary preacher needs to be very careful when choosing models of Christ. It may not be wise to shake a story loose of its historical moorings. What counts as a grace or a virtue changes over time.

St Francis sees a leper coming and dismounts from his horse and kisses him. It's a powerful story but verging on the bizarre. St Cuthbert stands in the North Sea up to his neck praying all night long. When he emerges in the morning the otters lick him dry and make him warm. It isn't just that you can't get the otters these days. Up to your neck in the North Sea? I don't think so.

Third, even when the stories do not seem strange and exotic, they can give the impression that the Christian faith belongs only to the past. I am profoundly moved by the martyrdom of Polycarp but it happened hundreds of years ago. William Temple, Hilda of Whitby, Dietrich Bonhoeffer, Trevor Huddleston, Brother Lawrence, Emil Brunner, Julian of Norwich, Thomas Cranmer – too many stories from the past and you give the impression that the Christian faith belongs to another time and place. I'm not suggesting that we never use examples drawn from the testimony of those who lived out the faith in previous centuries – where would preachers be without St Francis and C. S. Lewis? – but I am advocating balance. It doesn't help if a sermon never gets nearer to our time than 1945. It just makes people think: 'This has little to do with me because this lot all died in some other century.'

Finally, even when the story concerns a great Christian living today it still runs the danger of implying that Christianity is lived out primarily by celebrities. Martin Luther King and Mother Teresa can still illustrate how the gospel takes over a life. But they don't seem to inhabit my world. Even those who might make the papers or the Christian paperbacks today – Cliff Richard, Charles Colson, Jackie Pullinger, Jonathan Edwards, Aled Jones – live glamorous lives, they have more than their 15 minutes of fame on television and might even make an appearance on *Songs of Praise*.

Now the vision of goodness is not to be spurned. The famous can still show us how the gospel is to be lived out in the world. I want to hear about Sheila Cassidy and James Mawdsley. I want to see how even in the most desperate circumstances God's power can be manifested. Such stories have always nurtured discipleship; holding the possibility of faithful living before my eyes encourages and strengthens me. I accept that Albert Schweitzer is not much use to a teenager thinking about a career, but in small doses his story can still teach and inspire.

## MORE WHOLEMEAL BREAD AND LESS CAKE

Nevertheless, I also need to hear how the grace of God can be embodied in what ordinary people do. So my main plea in this chapter is for a greater use of stories, testimonies and accounts which come from real people living real lives.

I once followed a car which had a sticker in the rear window – 'People like you are turning to Christ'. It made me think whether it was more irritating than a Bible text or 'Baby on board'. But whatever your feelings about stickers, the idea seemed to be 'You could be like that.' The principle of using real stories of real people is that the life of faith becomes recognizable. The congregation thinks, 'That could be me. I could do that with my gifts', 'I'm struggling with a problem just like that', 'That person responded to an opportunity which is pretty much the same as the one that's opening up for me.' Such accounts and testimonies work because we recognize the central character as living in our world. They carry the strong message that the life of faith is do-able; that what the person in the pew is feeling is not unusual or peculiar. Even failure or doubt or loss of faith become experiences that can be named and handled through the stories of ordinary people who have or are going through difficult times. Most of the stories of great saints are stories of triumph. Stories of real people living in our world are less fantastical but they smell of real life.

Here are two examples of how accounts look when they are used in sermons. In the first excerpt the preacher is trying to embody the idea that we should bear one another's burdens:

Life had been going along smoothly for the Colburns until two family crises hit. First the Colburns' elder son was involved in a hit-and-run accident and arrested for driving under the influence, and then within two months their younger son was caught experimenting with drugs. The members of the prayer group recognized that the Colburns were embarrassed but one said, 'We wouldn't let them pull away. We knew that they couldn't get through this alone.' If the Colburns missed a Tuesday night, somebody would call. Letty Colburn said, 'We have been held up and carried by them. No one had done that before. They carried us through.'[4]

In this excerpt, Fleming Rutledge makes personal the idea that thankfulness can transform life. She has undertaken, rather reluctantly, to visit an old lady but is surprised at the outcome:

During the remaining years of her life I visited her and took care of many arrangements. To my surprise it became a pleasure and a joy, for this reason: she was incredibly grateful. Instead of complaining that I did not come often enough, she thanked me profusely for coming at all. She appreciated the little insignificant favours that I did for her as though they had been lavish gifts. When I dropped in for a few moments in between other commitments, you would have thought I was paying her a state visit. Her thankfulness created a new situation.[5]

Perhaps I can be forgiven for making two special pleas at this point. First, can we resolve to use more stories which focus on the workplace? I once heard a lecture by Mark Greene, Director of the London Institute for Contemporary Christianity. He asked provocatively, 'Who are your heroes?' It made me think how often our heroes are either dead Christians or people working triumphantly in areas like the mission field, evangelism or the Church. But most people spend most of their time in the world of work. Is the life of faith do-able in that bruising environment? Testimonies which deal with the workplace speak powerfully about the value and importance of our daily work. Above all, they earth our Christian discipleship in the real world.[6]

The second concerns truth. The 'Life' of St Confitura was a joke. But many genuine traditional accounts had a very loose connection with the truth. One medieval biographer said, 'It is difficult, *though not impossible*, to write the life of a saint about whom one knows absolutely nothing.' For him, writing about saints was all about *instructing* the reader. In other words, 'Never mind the truth, feel the improving message.' Unfortunately, the slogan is alive and well – and this bothers me. It may have been fine for preachers in the Middle Ages not to care if what they wrote really happened, but it won't do for us. Alas, I've heard several versions of the same story floating around in sermons but attached to different people. We ought not to be so casual about the facts.

## FIRST FIND YOUR SHOE BOX

The decision to use more examples drawn from the life of ordinary people soon runs into a problem. Where am I to find the stories? There are thousands of books devoted to the lives of the good and the famous. Very few describe the ordinary. We need to be on the lookout for examples. In time we may build up a shoe box full of cards which contain a testimony or an account which is not more than a paragraph long, which can be introduced relatively quickly and which captures some aspect of the life of faith. I confess that I have come late to this task and the shoe box is mainly in my mind.

There are two possible sources of material. First, our normal involvement in the life of the Church will supply us with a number of examples. There is an ethical issue here, of course. It is not acceptable to vacuum up people's problems in order to find sermon illustrations. It smacks too much of tickling the congregation's curiosity. But we need not exaggerate the problem. Most of the stories we want to use are not going to be about matters that are seriously confidential. They are more likely to be about people coping, working, believing, persisting or trying to express their faith in real, though undramatic, ways. Many will be happy for us to use their story provided we slightly disguise their identity and change the odd detail. And I have often made up an identikit account which consists of details which are true to life but not all to be found in the life of any one person. In the following excerpt all the facts, experiences and attitudes are true but the character is an amalgam of a number of people, not all from the same church or even from the same period of my life. The stories are fleshing out the idea that God does speak to us today through his Word.

Joanna goes to a small group but seldom says anything. She is tongue-tied because everyone else knows so much. She feels awkward and ignorant when they know how to find Obadiah without looking at the index. Long words like 'sanctification' terrify her. So she sits on the edge of the group and learns second hand. This Lent the group decided to study a book together and one morning she read a section and God spoke to her through it. It was nothing profound but it was something true and personal. She went to her group and thought, 'God has spoken to me, I mustn't keep silent.' So she shared what she'd heard in secret. No one laughed. To her amazement, everyone listened intently and at the end two people said, 'I found that really helpful.' Jesus gave her a word and she found her voice.

Mary is involved in her church in all kinds of ways – catering, leadership, sick visiting. It was during a perfectly ordinary sermon that she heard God calling her to preach. 'I don't do that sort of thing,' she thought. But God said, 'If I speak to you then you can tell others what you've heard.' She tested the call, giving one or two short reflections at a mid-week Communion service. She discovered that she really did have gifts of communication and is now training as a lay preacher. Jesus gave her a word and she found her voice.

A second source of testimonies and accounts can be found in books and magazine articles. I have found that *Gideon News* and *Alpha News* are full of examples which need relatively little editing. Of course, *Gideon News* tends to focus on people who have found a Gideon Bible at some crisis point in their life and *Alpha News* concentrates on the Alpha course, but both are strong on potted biographies and snapshots of key incidents. Just occasionally the daily paper will throw up treasure hidden in a field. Imagine my joy when I picked up the *Daily Telegraph* for 27 June 2001, a newspaper not known for its sensational reporting. I read that a blind grandmother drove a car at 140 m.p.h. around Brand's Hatch to raise money for the restoration of a church in Ramsgate. My imagination was tweaked and the piece found a place in a sermon on God who makes all things new and calls us to do daring things in his name:

Can't you hear the conversation at the Autumn Fete Committee? The vicar is looking for volunteers. 'Will you be making some of your loganberry pies this year, Mrs Fortescue, in aid of the church restoration appeal?' 'No Vicar, I shall not,' comes the firm response, 'but I will drive a car at 140 m.p.h. around Brand's Hatch – provided my guide dog can sit in the passenger seat next to me.' This is an icon for me of the sheer panache of the people of God once the God who makes all things new gets hold of them.

---

### EXERCISE

*Here is a list of general concepts to do with the Christian life. They could appear in any sermon. In their present form they are like insubstantial wraiths lacking a body. The task is to think of a story of a real person in a recognizably contemporary situation who will illustrate the idea. Ideally, you will remember, we want a testimony or an account which is not more than a paragraph long, which can be introduced relatively quickly and which captures this aspect of the life of faith.*

*The concepts are:*

- *Experiencing serious suffering yet managing to stay cheerful and positive.*
- *The cost of discipleship.*
- *Exercising power in a responsible way so as not to demean or destroy the weak or vulnerable.*
- *Integrity and honesty.*
- *Faithful service without making a fuss about it.*
- *The body of Christ.*

---

When preachers try this exercise they usually end up telling one another wonderful stories of unheard-of saints. It makes you feel good to bring to people's imagination some individual who has embodied an aspect of the Christian life. And it is never time wasted to celebrate the glories of God's multi-coloured grace and the saints who will never appear in the collections of 'inspiring stories'. When preaching on 'honesty and integrity' I have sometimes used the following story:

Such people are enormously attractive. I once taught a little Quaker girl who went into the Sixth Form and studied for her A levels. In the autumn of her second year she went for interview to a very prestigious university. The interviewer came from hell. He sat with his feet on the desk, smoking, looking out of the window, and picking holes in her answers. Eventually he asked: 'So, what do you look for in a newspaper?' She gave the best answer she could manage. 'Huh' was the reply. Then, 'What do you think I look for in a newspaper?' She sweetly replied, 'Spelling mistakes and grammatical errors.' You could bet on always getting a straight answer from her. I think this core of integrity and straight talking came from her Quaker upbringing and a family which expected her to speak the truth. She went to Sussex University in the end.

# 10 What would you do?

*Dilemmas and case studies*

The parables of Jesus show that it is possible to preach without being explicit about the meaning of the message. Jesus clearly thought that people were capable of working away at a parable for themselves. The dilemma or case study has the same purpose – to embody the word in a recognizable situation and leave the ending open for the listener to supply.

The following vignette is taken from a conference workbook. It invites solutions to Billy's problem. Why is he unsettled in his church? What different courses of action can he take? What would you recommend him to do?

> I have been going to a very active church for a number of years now and have got a lot from it. I used to be involved in leading some of the children's work but I gave that up recently since I felt it was time to move on to something else. I am a bit unsettled in the church at the moment since I no longer have a clear role. My best friend is very involved – recently he was asked on to the elders' court and has agreed to this. He is very committed to a number of things in the church and clearly gets a lot out of this involvement. Sometimes I feel he is too busy to notice my situation. I go to church faithfully but I find I am getting less and less from the sermons. The minister is a good man but we have never had a meaningful relationship so I could not bring myself to speak to him about how I am feeling. I feel I am slipping in my faith and beginning to find church a struggle.[1]

The case study was designed for a discussion group but when I saw it I thought it had mileage for preachers. Sermons characteristically tell people things. There is no lack of information or exhortation. Is there a sermon design which aims to provoke questions without hurrying on to answers – or even stops short of the answers? The dilemma is intended to encourage congregations to work at the solution for themselves.

What is to count as a dilemma?[2] In essence it is a case study involving a single character in a recognizably realistic setting. This character is confronted with a conflict of values and ideals, so that a range of options is open to them, each one involving a decision and consequent action. The sermon which uses a dilemma framework engages congregations since it offers different scenarios and invites them to weigh up alternative courses of action. It feels like, 'Let's discuss this situation together', even though only the preacher is speaking. Hearers are put in the position of having to take sides, decide on options and make choices.

Take for example, this case study devised by James Lawrence in a book on evangelism:

> 'What did you do over the weekend?' asks Sylvia. Imagine Sylvia asks this question on Monday morning. This is a potential opportunity. Although in some circumstances answering a question with a question is appropriate – Jesus was brilliant at it – in this instance it doesn't appear to be the right response. Sylvia expects an answer to her question . . . [3]

In a sermon this case study allows the preacher to range across the possibilities. The responses might be crassly insensitive ('I was in the House of God which is where you ought to be each Sunday if you don't wish to perish eternally') or embarrassed and ineffective ('Err, um, nothing much, can't really remember'). They might be aggressive ('What do you want to know for, nosey?') or factual ('We went to church in the morning'). Lawrence himself explores some answers to Sylvia's question:

> If we respond, 'I went to church, would you like to come?' what is her likely reaction? A polite person may say, 'Um, no thank you' and internally be thinking, 'Religious nutter.'
>
> We can hazard a guess that she thinks church is dull, boring and irrelevant, so we could say, 'On Sunday we did what we always do. We find it really enjoyable, and it sets us up for the rest of the week – we went to our church.'

Most dilemmas will appear as sections of a sermon. The preacher may range across the possibilities, trying to help the congregation to experience something of the conflict for themselves, before going on to choose one. Alternatively, the preacher may leave the options hanging, as it were, recognizing that the unresolved issue is likely to niggle away at the mind more than a problem neatly tied up and packaged.

## ABIGAIL'S DILEMMAS

There seems no reason why we should not go one step further. Perhaps a dilemma could constitute the framework of the whole sermon. I haven't found any examples of this move yet, though I cannot see why it shouldn't be possible. So, as an experiment, I offer the following sermon as an illustration of how one might try to embody the central ideas in 2 Corinthians 6.3—7.1 through the medium of dilemmas. In this passage Paul urges his readers to accept the grace of God and declares that he is desperate not to put obstacles in anyone's way, so that no one can find fault with his ministry. He lists some of the ways in which he has commended himself as a servant of God. In the last six verses he exhorts the Corinthians to be holy and separate from unbelievers. Obstacles to faith, commending the gospel, remaining holy in the world – these are rich themes. I decided to turn them into Abigail's dilemmas.

We put no stumbling block in anyone's path so that the ministry will not be discredited. Let me introduce you to Abigail. She's in her thirties, holding down a good job, a responsible position, something to do with money in a big firm in Newcastle. She leads an active social life, some of it at the gym and health club; some, surprisingly to those who don't know her well, at line dancing. She watches TV, as you do – *ER*, *Cold Feet*, *The West Wing* – and catches a film most weeks. She's got a decent collection of CDs – no Des O'Connor. One high spot in her life is the regular girlies' night out with about half a dozen friends. She has a boyfriend – John. He's interested in her and she's fond of him. They go walking together at weekends, visit the Baltic and he's got GSOH. And along with all this – Abigail has a strong faith in Christ.

Churches are full of Abigails. She lives in two worlds. One is the world of the Church (services, home group) and the other the world she shares with her friends and colleagues. It's a bit of a balancing act, and living in two worlds constantly presents her with decisions. It gets wearing sometimes. It would be good to have some guiding principles – like those in the Bible passage.

There is an easy option. Pull out of the secular world and go for total separation. Retire into the safe ghetto of the Church. Pull up the drawbridge and let down the portcullis. Tape up the windows so that no poison gas from the world can contaminate her faith. So she dumps the girlies' night out and the line dancing. The cinema visits disappear and she watches only nature documentaries on television. Unfortunately the net result is that she can forget evangelism. She has a kind of holiness but has lost her contacts.

A second option is to jump into the world and go for total immersion. She becomes indistinguishable from everyone else – at work, in her social life and with John. She knocks off at 4.50 because everyone else does, photocopies several hundred pages a month for her own use, and uses the firm's phone for long private conversations with John. Taking to this option with enthusiasm, she drinks more than everyone else and slags off her colleagues behind their backs. Things come to a head when a workmate discovers she goes to church and says, 'What, you a Christian! You can't be! You swear more than the rest of us.' The net result is that she can forget evangelism. She has maintained contacts but now has no credibility.

Pull out or jump in. Total separation or total immersion. No contacts or no credibility. Neither move seems to be working. Is there a third option?

This would be a possible point at which to invite the congregation to think of alternative courses of action. In some church contexts it might be possible to break into groups or receive comments from the congregation. Then the sermon could pick up the action with the preacher's own response to Abigail's situation.

Abigail reflects on 2 Corinthians 6. Maybe it isn't a matter of pull out or jump in but *stand out*. She starts to think more seriously about stumbling blocks. Paul's point is that God's ministers reflect on God. She recalls the old line: 'You are the only Bible some people will read.' So what is it that commends the gospel?

She's noticed that people are impressed when Christians handle pressure and problems with stickability and don't give up, when they keep their head in trying circumstances. So she tries to be consistent and persistent. It was a good moment when, at the end of a frantic day, with everyone blowing their top, the boss said, 'This has been a terrible day. You're the only one who hasn't gone ballistic at some point.'

Abigail is giving it a go. And people are impressed. They're impressed by plain honest goodness, by making a real effort to understand, alongside patience, kindness and telling the truth. People are also impressed by her openness. Abigail is not afraid to be herself or show affection. She tries not to hide herself behind a mask or a front.

People are impressed by something else. Perhaps 'intrigued' is closer to it. Abigail doesn't seem to be bothered whether she gets the approval and praise of others or not. It's as if she's dancing to a different tune. There's an integrity that is intriguing and mysterious. Now the prospects for evangelism look better. She has kept her contacts and her credibility.

That's where I feel like stopping. But it wouldn't be life if everything was perfect. So the plot thickens a bit.

An image that means a lot to Abigail is Paul's: 'You are a temple of the living God.' God lives in her. He fills her. He walks around her life so that the key of every room is open to him and he may go anywhere. The hospitality of her heart is given to God. He is the well-spring of her life. This is fulfilling and deeply satisfying. It is the source of that inner direction that her friends notice. It's wonderful but it causes lots of problems.

At work there are some practices which are not strictly ethical. It's not too difficult to cut corners. Abigail is uneasy about this. Cliques develop which jockey for influence and power. These alliances make her anxious. There's a particular inner circle of people who are seen as movers and shakers. She would like to be part of the group (and they are keen to welcome her) but bothered about their attitudes and practices. She expresses her unease and falls from favour. So she is no longer privy to those important but hush-hush discussions in lowered voices by the coffee machine. In fact, she is seen as a bit of a fuss-pot.

Social life is pretty good until the girls suggest an evening at a night club with a male stripper. It's just a bit of fun. Abigail's not crazy about the idea and cries off. The general reaction is, 'Oh, come on, relax! Lighten up!' Things get a bit tense and she is seen as a bit strait-laced.

She's as fond of John as ever she was. But he is pushing hard to sleep with her and is frankly bewildered why she won't oblige. She has problems with that. She cannot see how she can share with him at the deepest level. There is an intimacy which is not possible since the hospitality of the heart is given to Christ. Abigail is sad about this because she really likes him. They remain very good friends. She lives in hope and prays that one day he will come to faith.

Now I am going to stop – just at the interesting part. Can I leave it with some questions? What do you think is going to happen next? What would you like to happen? And what do you think ought to happen?

The sermon finishes with the problem left unanswered. It could be formally addressed by group discussion or a period of silent reflection or a prayer for the Abigails of this world. I do not think it is necessarily a fault for a sermon not to cross every 't' or dot every 'i'. I understand that when I preached this sermon half a dozen members of the congregation went to a coffee shop after the service and debated the issues for two hours. So the strategy can work in the right context.

Should we always tie up loose ends? What happens if people come to the wrong answer? Perhaps it is sometimes more important to keep the question open so that people work away at the situation for themselves. One preacher is sure that we avoid doing this.

We do not trust our listeners to negotiate the process on their own. We are afraid that they might not get it *right* so we pour a concrete bridge for them to walk across and the live synapse becomes a dead end. When we reduce stories to morals and turn parables into allegories, that is what we are doing. We are back into the old, old business of flattening out experience so that we can write advice all over it, making God and all creation yawn.[4]

## EXERCISE

*I am hesitant about including an exercise but was intrigued by the possibilities in this excerpt from Mark Greene's* Thank God It's Monday.

*'Larry is one of the leading lawyers in his field in the country. He leaves his house at about six-thirty every day, and he usually gets back by eight-thirty. He has a wife and three teenage children. He often leads worship in his home church. He preaches from time to time, administers a Trust and is involved in a variety of Christian ministries.*

*Does he have a life?'*[5]

*Devise a dilemma-type sermon using the snapshot of Larry. Include conflicts of values, press the issue, 'What should he do?' and try to explore the question, 'Does he have a life?'*

# 11 Everything went really well until Friday . . .

## Stories and illustrations

It would be foolish to attempt a book on embodying the Word and omit the embodying technique par excellence – telling a story. Narrative is so powerful and so natural a form for embodying truth that it will come in at every point in sermon design. The previous chapters all imply or employ story. For example, the *imaginative elaboration* of a biblical story takes a narrative form. *Images* are freeze-frames in the mind which have a story implicit within them, *instances* are tiny stories which have not yet started to move. *Testimonies* or *accounts* consist of instances which have grown into short stories, with greatly abbreviated characterization and plot. *Dilemmas* highlight a conflict experienced by a central character and invite more than one possible ending. What are loosely referred to as *illustrations* are, typically, extended narratives.

In *A Preaching Workbook*, I looked at stories as if they were unexploded bombs. I now feel I was rather grudging in my assessment. I know that, unless they are handled with great care, they can blow up in your face, but it is precisely because stories are so powerful that we cannot afford to leave them to the bomb-disposal experts.

Jesus used stories with skill and to great effect and most great preachers have followed his example. Long before people started talking about a visually oriented society or the story-shaped world, storytellers were entrancing their hearers with a well-told tale.[1]

And when it is done skilfully it can trigger profound reactions. I recently heard of a formidable secondary-school inspector telling the story of Christ's mocking to a lower set of 15-year-olds, who seemed not to have heard it before. When he came to the part about the crown of thorns, one of the boys exclaimed, quite genuinely, 'The bastards!' Most of us would settle for that reaction.

# WHAT IS A STORY?

I begin with the basic question. What is to count as a story? Stories move through time. We need characters to play their part in the narrative, a setting so that we can locate them somewhere and a series of linked events. However, these ingredients are not yet enough to turn the characters and the setting into a story. I overheard a woman telling her granddaughter 'a story'. It was about two kittens who put on their mittens and went for a walk in the forest. They spent some time together and then they came home for their tea. That hardly counts as a story. You might as well tell a story about taking the lid off a pot of paint and allowing it to evaporate.

Something needs to happen to the characters, the setting and the events to turn them into a story. At some point, the settled world of the opening scenes has to be disturbed. It is the complication that produces the story. Rather than a beginning, a middle and an end, we need a beginning, a muddle and an end. The unsettling element demands a resolution. How will it all end? What are they going to do now? How are they going to get out of this one? Are these kittens going to lose their mittens (having been told not to take them off by mummy cat)? Will they meet a wolf in the forest or fall into a bog? Something's going to have to happen to upset the applecart (to use Eugene Lowry's phrase) or we don't have a story.

There's much more to be said. To do justice to story we probably ought to mention narrator and narratee (and possibly implied narrator and implied narratee), plot, trajectory, characterization, flashbacks and many other technical terms. It is also true that in many stories the complication is implicit rather than expressed, so that some narratives move through a sequence of setting and development straight to revelation and surprise. But I am primarily interested in those narratives where the still surface of the opening scene is troubled. This moment seizes the interest of the listeners. How is this complication going to be resolved? They suspect that somehow it *will* be resolved, or they will feel cheated, and that 'somehow' will keep them engaged until the dénouement.

# MUDDYING THE WATERS

Settings are usually straightforward and resolutions will follow because you already have some idea of what this story has to do and therefore where it has to go. Very often it's the complication which is both crucial and difficult in sermon design. It will demand creative thought on the part of the preacher unless it's already built into the story.

Something has to introduce tension into the story. Something has to surprise or puzzle or scandalize us. Maybe it tweaks our curiosity by promising more. Conflict is a standard way of complicating the plot. Even as artless a phrase as: 'Everything went really well until Friday . . .' can do the trick.

It may be useful to set out some of the words we use when we are pointing towards the complicating phase of a narrative:

- *Suspense* is the artful withholding of information and its slow release. It's like waiting for the second shoe to drop on the floor of the bedroom above.
- *Disequilibrium* is the equivalent of balancing precariously on one leg hoping you might get back on two feet (but who knows?).
- *Tension* splits the plot so that one part pulls against the other and the listener's allegiance is pulled taut.
- *Muddle* describes the feeling of 'I thought I could see clearly to the bottom of the pond and then somebody stirred up the silt'.
- *Blind alleys* and *false leads* evoke the question: 'Why do we keep taking the wrong turning?' The expected end is frustrated by complications. It's the experience of the maze as you approach the centre.
- *Concealment* points to the feeling that something is being deliberately hidden. 'What's behind the curtain and why won't she let us see it? When's the unveiling?'.
- *Torque* evokes the idea of tightening the spring and the sense that 'I can't stand much more of this – something is going to go pop'. It's the horror film's 'Just as you thought it was safe to come out . . .'.
- *Discrepancy* marks the gap between what is and what ought to be, or what I want and what is actually happening. We want something to bridge the gap.
- *Unease* describes the feeling that everything seems to be going well but something still doesn't feel quite right.
- The *cliffhanger* is the classic soap technique. The story reaches the point of no return, the plot is at the edge of the abyss, hanging on by its fingertips.

These terms embrace such plot devices as delay, ambiguity, incompleteness, chaos, surprise and conflict. We need to ensure that our storytelling employs them at the critical phase in the narrative, otherwise we forfeit the crucial element. If the listeners walk round stories like people at an exhibition then we can be sure that they will disappear to the tea room when they have seen it all. We must try not to give them the freedom to wander at will. A colleague said of sermons: 'Even when I am about to drift away, one phrase will always pull me back. It's something like: "A strange thing happened to me last week . . ."' In other words, the complicating element in the story will engage the listener every time.

---

### EXERCISE

*To earth this principle, you might like to try inserting a complicating factor into a story. Tell the story of your day. This could easily become a list of events and encounters, like a diary entry. Now shape part of the narrative so that it has a setting, a complication and a resolution. Try to impose the same structure on your last sermon (assuming that it wasn't already in this form).*

---

One of the results of this exercise is that it demonstrates that any experience can turn into a story. Books on preaching sometimes discuss the best sources for story illustrations, but the fact is that stories may be quarried from anywhere. The Bible, personal life, the newspapers, the TV soap or drama or news, magazines, the world of the film and the novel all provide us with stories. Then there are books of stories: collections of sermon illustrations (though these are often like Saul's armour – one size doesn't fit all); stories set in far-off lands and ancient times or in a timeless mythical setting ('There was once a princess who could not sleep . . .'); stories of old monks and wise rabbis and stories of ghastly, spiritually precocious, unlocalized, untraceable, unlikeable children who come out with sentimental observations about God and life.

But what makes them stories is that they have a setting, a complication and a resolution.

## THE STORY-SHAPED WORD

What are stories good for? The narrative form is a compelling way of embodying spiritual ideas.

### 1. Turning a doctrine into a story

It was said that George Whitefield taught the key doctrines of Christianity mainly through the medium of stories. Many doctrines began life as stories but we think of theology as extracting truth from word pictures and clarifying it in propositions. In the Gospels we tend to find the reverse process going on. Long before Paul wrote about justification, Jesus had encapsulated the doctrine in the story of the Pharisee and Publican. The story leads us into revelation and surprise. The setting is briefly described. The hearers assume that the Pharisee is a model worshipper. The publican's prayer reinforces their assumption. And the last line turns their world upside down.

### 2. Turning an exhortation into a story

Hebrews 12.3 contains the exhortation: 'Consider him . . . so that you may not grow weary or lose heart . . . You have not yet resisted to the point of shedding your blood.' Exhortations can fall on deaf ears, as we all know. Narrative turns the command into a moving picture in which we are participants.

> Look at him. He could have had an easy life but set his face like a flint to follow the course to the end. He endured the cross, despising the shame. Consider him so that you do not grow weary and lose heart.
>
> There is a *via dolorosa* in Jerusalem. Pilgrims follow it through winding streets and alleyways. Someone will often carry a cross because the road leads to Calvary. Look at Jesus now as he walks this road. Jesus – the man who followed this path through humiliation, shame and pain. I catch a glimpse of his face. There's blood running from the crown of thorns, bruises on the cheek bones, sweat and exhaustion. He falls under the weight. And gets to his feet, staggering on, gripped, nailed to the promise of God that this is the course that leads to glory.

I step into the road and say to him, 'I find faith gets in the way of my interests, my entertainment, my leisure, my holidays. Being a disciple doesn't always give me what I need.' As I speak, he looks at me. Some words of St Francis come to mind: 'If I am to complain, let me complain to Christ on the cross.' And I fall silent. Consider him so that you do not grow weary and lose heart. You have not yet resisted to the point of shedding your blood.

## GETTING IN BY THE BACK DOOR

Narrative is an indirect form of preaching. It doesn't poke a finger into people's faces. It invites the congregation to stand at the preacher's side, not square up to him or her. The tale of Nathan and David demonstrates how a story can get behind a listener's defences. The story has an existence apart from the prophet and this allows a sensitive issue to be handled safely. Stories get under the skin.

Joe McKeever, the pastor of First Baptist Church of Kenner, Louisiana, speaks of story as a way of preaching controversial issues without making people mad. He maintains that this is the way to preach 'Hot Potatoes'. How do you confront without affront? He tells a story:

I came by the technique by accident. I stopped at a family-style restaurant one time and as I was seated, two older fellows brought their trays and sat across from me. One man engaged me in conversation, the other was silent. We talked about the governor's race and the segregationist candidate whom he supported. 'Tell me one verse in the Bible that condemns segregation,' the old man said to me. As I swallowed and prepared a response, the silent partner spoke up: 'Love thy neighbour as thyself.'[2]

McKeever observes: 'I've told the story in great detail many times, and I always let the quiet man make my point for me.'

## THE VIEW FROM OVER HERE

It isn't just delicate issues which can be handled through narrative. Story is particularly effective at showing us truths in new perspective, especially when the truths are familiar. The congregation feels that it's heard all this before and mentally switches off. That's when story comes into its own. We all learn early on to protect ourselves from words, but story shows us ourselves from another angle, like catching a glimpse of our reflection from the side in a full-length mirror.

One of my favourite examples is a story by Kierkegaard about geese. We can harangue the congregation about not really believing and acting on the faith we proclaim week by week, but this story sneaks up on you.

Try to imagine for a moment that geese could talk – that they had so arranged things that they too had their divine worship and their church-going. Every Sunday they would meet together and a gander would preach.

The sermon was essentially the same each time – it told of the glorious destiny of geese, of the noble end for which their maker had created them – and every time his name was mentioned all the geese curtsied and all the ganders bowed their heads. They were to use their wings to fly away to the distant pastures to which they really belonged; for they were only pilgrims on this earth.

The same thing happened each Sunday. Thereupon the meeting broke up and they all waddled home, only to meet again the following Sunday for divine worship and waddle off home again – but that was as far as they ever got. They throve and grew fat, plump and delicious – and at Michaelmas they were eaten – and that was as far as they ever got. It never came to anything. For while their conversation on Sundays was all high-sounding, on Mondays they would tell each other what had happened to the goose who had taken the end set before them quite seriously, and in spite of many tribulations had tried to use the wings its creator had bestowed upon it . . .

Among the geese were several who looked ill and wan, and all the other geese said, 'There, you see what comes of taking flying seriously. It is all because they go about meditating on flying that they get thin and wan and are not blessed by the grace of God as we are; for that is why we grow fat, plump and delicious.'

And so next Sunday off they went to divine service, and the old gander preached of the glorious end for which their Maker (and at that point all the geese curtsied and all the ganders bowed their heads) had created them, and of why they were given wings.[3]

## THE MANY ROLES OF STORY

I have argued that stories can help us see ideas as they are embodied in people and situations, can help us face up to ideas which are disturbing, and freshen up ideas that have grown stale and lifeless. But a story can perform many other roles within the total structure of a sermon.

For example, a story can introduce the sermon, setting up a way of looking at the world which the preacher will attack in the complicating phase. Or a story can embody the complication by conflicting with some widely accepted 'truth'. Sometimes it can pose a problem for us because we feel, 'It just can't be so!' On another occasion, the preacher can get cross with the story or take its side and agonize along the lines of 'If that story is true, then how can we go on doing this?' At the end of the sermon a story can supply the resolution or *dénouement*. Any story can play all these roles, but biblical stories will often play them especially well.[4]

A sermon on the parable of the Talents illustrates this technique. William Willimon appears to preach against Jesus. For example, he spends a lot of time defending the little man who we think should have been the hero. He tells us that we were right to identify 'with the little guy who makes good'. After retelling the story he praises the servant's prudence and ethical response – after all, he keeps his master's money safe and, in any case, it's not his to play around with. The speech put into the servant's mouth reflects what we are feeling:

> Here master, you gave me one talent. Here's your one talent back. All safe and sound. I didn't waste any of it. Didn't risk any of it. Didn't blow it on any crackpot business schemes or loan it to any of my cronies.

Just to make it clear that Willimon is taking issue with Jesus he underlines the point:

> We do not like this story. The little guy just got clobbered for doing what was right, for doing what was prudent, for doing what we would have done. We do not like this story.

It's not until the last page that Willimon probes whether this master is hard-hearted or soft-headed or generous:

> Or is he an extravagant, reckless wheeler-dealer, whose faith in his servants is exceeded only by his generosity? He gave them all that he had. Every cent. Is it hard-hearted of him to expect them to be as reckless as he? And when they come back to render account, you'd think that, if he is pleased, he might let them keep some of the interest they have earned. No, he tells them to keep it all, interest and principal.[5]

The hearers have to wait until the end before Willimon shows that the master may be a sloppy businessman but he models the generosity of God and the way he is prepared to trust us and risk everything on us.

## THE NARRATIVE SERMON

For the sake of completeness I should mention that the whole sermon may take the form of one story. An earlier chapter has dealt with retelling Bible stories, here I want to illustrate how the sermon can itself take the form of an extended narrative.

A sermon on Acts 16.1–15 opens up the concept of God calling, leading and guiding us. It began by dealing with the dispute between Paul and Barnabas, the choice of Silas and Timothy and the strengthening and encouragement of the churches in Galatia. This much is scene setting. The complicating phase begins when the immediate work is done. Do Paul and his team return home? This is unthinkable when the whole dynamic of the story is to move on in the power of the Spirit. But where to? They try the obvious road to Ephesus and the Spirit says 'No'. They try to enter Bithynia and the Spirit blocks that move. They contemplate Mysia but pass it by. The plot is now in confusion and comes to a climax at Troas:

> The land has run out and there's nowhere else to go. So Troas it is. But nobody stops at Troas – it's like Stranraer or Holyhead or Dover. But beyond? That means the sea and unknown parts where dragons live. Can we put ourselves into their shoes? They have ignored every sensible and obvious move. They have travelled

without knowing what they're doing it for. The narrative drives them to Troas. 'We've come across Asia from south east to north west and no new evangelism, no new churches set up. Opportunity after opportunity has gone begging. And we've done this for over 300 miles. The voices in our heads are saying that it's all folly.'

Having set up the problem, the sermon moves swiftly to a resolution like that of the biblical narrative – with the voyage to Philippi and the conversion of Lydia. But the emphasis lies on the journey into the unknown. The sermon ends like this:

Does God guide? Paul would have said, 'Of course he does – confusingly, unpredictably, but faithfully and unerringly, for his glory and our good.' 'Of course God guides,' says Paul. 'It was easy at the beginning when we were getting ourselves ready to be guided and it was fantastic at the end when we saw face to face the first Christian convert in Europe. It's just the bit in the middle that was tricky.'

Stories represent a powerful way of embodying the Word. Properly shaped, they can change lives. But they remain open and preserve the listener's right to dissent. This is their nature and it is part of their attractiveness. Matthew implies that Jesus used stories with the crowds in order to tease out thought and address the whole person. This means that it is always possible for people to reject the tension which you have so lovingly set up. They can disengage from the questions the story asks of them. I remember the graffiti on a student noticeboard: 'Frodo, chuck the ring and go and get drunk.' At least one person was bored of the Rings.

# 12 Telling the very old, old story

*Preaching and parables*

There is one category of story which deserves a chapter all to itself. The problems which buzz around when preaching on any familiar Bible story become acute when preaching on parables. Modern congregations cannot hear parables as they were first preached. There is no sudden revelation which disturbs the settled world. We know the boy will come home, the coin will be found and the foolish bridesmaids locked out. A colleague who works with international students, who are unfamiliar with the Bible, rightly reminded me that in that context the parables are still dynamite. But for the average congregation it is difficult to build tension and no one goes home scandalized.

There are at least three kinds of difficulty. First, how are we to *preserve the puzzling nature of parables*? Many parables were spoken as riddles. Their point was not obvious. They were examples of 'telling it slant', inviting the hearers to wrestle with the meaning, puzzle away and return to the parable again and again. How can they be preached when the task of the contemporary preacher is seen as *explaining* the parable? Clearly explained, the parable loses its capacity to annoy us for the rest of the week. Will congregations stand for being left baffled and puzzled at the end of the sermon?

Second, how are we to *retain the tension and suspense of a parable whose ending we know*? The familiarity of the parables is the major barrier to hearing them as they were first heard. We know the ending. Even if someone in the church didn't know the ending, we read the story in the Gospels right through to the end before preaching on it! Tension and suspense evaporate. Parables lose their 'teasing' nature. They should be 'narrative snares', producing complacency and then suddenly biting the listener. How can the preacher reproduce the shock of hearing for the first time the Good Samaritan, the Labourers in the Vineyard or the Prodigal Son?

Third, how are we to *communicate the surprising nature of God and the kingdom*? Parables present a topsy-turvy world, which by familiarity with the Christian tradition we find hard to feel first hand. We are not surprised or scandalized or fascinated by the vision. We have taken the strange world of Jesus and learned to live with it, domesticating its subversive nature. How can the sermon create again the shocking, amazing and deeply attractive nature of the world Jesus offers?

In summary then, parables today are not puzzling because sermons make their meaning clear; they lack all tension because the hearers know the ending; they do not shock or surprise because we have learned to live with the paradoxes. These three problems all raise the question of how we are to ensure that the parable is a contemporary and self-involving word.

As we have them, parables belong to the past. They were originally designed to be self-involving. They aimed not so much at understanding as changed lives and conversion. They were meant to challenge people, to address, engage and involve them. And they achieved this effect by drawing the listener into the world of the parable. Stories of people in situations are addictive. We should find ourselves addressed, taking sides, identifying, delivering a verdict. But is it possible for stories which the congregation knows inside out to get under the skin?

How can the preacher best respond to the peculiar difficulties posed by parables? Here are six possible strategies.

## 1. Retell the parable but in a fresh way

This first method intends that the congregation will re-experience the story. Most will not hear it as if they'd never heard it before but they may hear it in a way analogous to a theatre audience which goes to a new production of *King Lear* or *A Midsummer Night's Dream*. The Bible story remains the same but the fresh retelling will help the congregation to hear new things. There will be tension and suspense but they will not reside in the story so much as in the preacher's telling of it. After all, though some may have heard the story of the Wise Men hundreds of times, they haven't heard it the way you tell it. In your version of the story the Wise Men might not make it to Bethlehem.

Well, they almost certainly will but the view from the top of the camel will be different.

Here's a retelling of the parable of the Yeast in Matthew 13.33. It's one verse in the Gospel but the preacher lovingly works on the retelling, expanding it here, modernizing there, putting in lots of pauses, reflecting the passage of time with expression and gesture with the result that the congregation hears the old story in a new way.

Yeast doesn't look like much. The woman takes the yeast and mixes it into the flour. She adds water, some sugar to feed the yeast and she stirs. She adds salt and mixes some more. She turns out the dough onto the work surface and kneads and pummels and stretches. Then she puts the dough back into the bowl, covers it with a tea-towel and leaves it somewhere warm. And she waits and she waits. Nothing seems to be happening. She vacuums the kitchen. She goes to the neighbour's for coffee. She does the *Guardian* crossword – well, half of it. And she waits. Nothing seems to be happening. There is just a hint of a delicious, yeasty smell in the air. But still she has to wait. And yet all this time the yeast is working, tiny bubbles are stretching the dough, causing it to change shape and expand and fill the bowl, and by the time the woman comes back the dough has pushed the tea-towel off the bowl and has covered the work surface. The process takes time, it takes patience but at the end of the afternoon the kitchen smells wonderful and the reward is amazing.[1]

## 2. Incorporate fresh insight into the background of the story

The preacher told us that the servant in the parable of the Unforgiving Servant owed the king 10,000 talents. We barely stirred. But he'd done his homework. 'I'll give you some idea of the vast amount involved,' he said and informed us that the total tax revenue collected from Judaea, Samaria and Idumea in one whole year had been calculated at only 600 talents. 'And how many denarii are there in one talent?' he asked. We had no idea. '6,000 denarii in one talent.' And a denarius is the equivalent of a day's wage. So the servant had been let off a total of 60 million denarii, a vast sum, beyond imagination. He cried out to the king, 'Give me time and I'll pay.' We found this laughable; he could never possibly pay back such a sum. In fact the interesting question for us was what he'd been doing to run up a debt of that size. To the servant's amazement (and ours) the king said, 'I'll forget it. I'll let it drop. I won't hold it against you.' 'Now,' said the preacher, 'if you'd just been forgiven 60 million denarii, you'd surely forgive someone who owed you a mere hundred?'

In this way some unpromising material about monetary values in the Ancient World gave us a new hearing of a familiar story.

### 3. Change the point of view

The congregation may have a new experience when it hears a parable from the perspective of a character within it. Maybe having to handle an over-familiar story is the main motivation of preachers who adopt a first-person stream of consciousness. A sermon by John Vannorsdall which takes the viewpoint of the elder brother in the Prodigal Son (Luke 15) offers a star-tling, compassionate but ultimately challenging hearing of the story.[2]

> Year after year preachers great and small, in a hundred languages,
> lead you from the bathos of my younger brother's self-imposed exile
> to the sounds of dancing and leave you staring at me, disgusted
> because I will not share the celebration for the prodigal's return.
> It's time you heard my side of the story.

Vannorsdall is not content just to reset the point of view, however. As the sermon proceeds, he moves our attention into the 'elder brother syndrome' in life and in the Church.

> There are those who come to a party, and there are those who
> work to prepare for that party, who see to it that the house is clean,
> that there is enough wine, that the fire is well built and that the
> musicians are ready. There are those who go home from the party
> singing their happy songs, and there are those of us who clean up
> after them, who sweep the cracker crumbs and bits of smoked fish
> from the floor and wipe the white circles left by the mugs on the
> polished wood.

Finally in a poignant section the preacher asks the question:

> How shall we be saved, we elder brothers and sisters? How can we go
> home when we are already home? How can we confess the squan-
> dering of resources, the harlots, the months and years of neglect,
> when in fact we have built and not squandered, not gone with
> harlots, and been responsible for preserving the family fortunes?

This technique draws the listeners in, involves them in the story and leads them to find the elder brother in themselves.

## 4. Use the parable to scandalize the congregation

When a parable is well known, the preacher cannot rely on its surprise value. But it can still be used in a provocative way. The preacher may use the story to dig a deeper and deeper hole. The tension then arises from the question, 'So how's the preacher going to get out of this one?' or even, 'How is Jesus going to get out of this one?'

We can see this happening in the parable of the Labourers in the Vineyard (Matthew 20.1–16). The story begins innocently enough, with labourers being hired at different points in the day. In the evening the owner asks his foreman to call the workmen and pay them. The first note of suspense comes in the remark '. . . beginning with the last ones hired and going on to the first'. We sense a teasing hint that something is up and are intrigued to see why the owner wants the wages given out in reverse order. The surprise comes next when those hired at the eleventh hour receive the full amount, exactly as was promised to those hired first. We are left thinking, 'If this is so, however much will those who have worked all day get then?' The plot thickens yet more when those who have worked through the heat of the day also end up with a denarius – just as the owner promised, but now not at all what they expected. The spring is tightened yet further by their outburst: 'You have made these men (sniff) equal to us.'

How will the owner (and Jesus) get out of this? The parable ends with the punch line: 'Are you miffed because I'm generous?' This ends the parable but doesn't solve the problem. For many congregations, things are now worse. They are left with a clear conflict between what is just and the provocative behaviour of the owner (now aggravated by Jesus' support). The preacher can preserve the tension by sharpening up the unfairness of it all, tightening the spring by taking the side of the disaffected workmen and by drawing parallels with church life. Unconsciously we identify with those who have worked all day – after all, we are the ones who come to services, run home groups, give money, make quiches, organize coffee mornings and collect for Christian Aid. The parable can do its work of scandalizing the listeners even though they all know the ending from the beginning.

Can the tension be resolved? One way of doing so is to use a question suggested by Fred Craddock many years ago: 'Where are you standing within the text?' What happens if the preacher moves the position of the congregation?

Will you ask yourself: 'At what time of day was I hired? Am I the worker hired at the end of the day? Did it even enter my head that I might be? But I *am* one of those hired at the eleventh hour. I'm no great catch, a pretty ordinary Christian. I wasn't there at 9 o'clock when Augustine and the Archbishop of Canterbury clocked in. I'm not Mother Teresa or Billy Graham or St Francis. I'm not Ned Flanders or the Reverend Lovejoy. I'm not even Cliff Richard or Mel Gibson. And God pours his grace and good gifts into my life. And gives me much, much more than I deserve.' Now, that really isn't fair. But it's wonderful.

## 5. Tell a different story with the same shape and force of the original parable

There's a magnificent sermon by Jerry Camery-Hoggatt on the Good Samaritan which begins memorably, 'Now let me tell you why I'm not going to preach on this text this morning.'[3] The Good Samaritan must be one of those nightmare passages where we feel that everything that can be said has been said. Camery-Hoggatt cleverly tells a story of a time when he drove past a group of migrant workers trying to mend a flat tyre on a country road. As he does so he is working on a sermon on the Good Samaritan and tries to fix in his imagination the details of the scene. Migrant workers, maybe illegal aliens, might be a good parallel to the Samaritan. The following day he is travelling the same road and breaks down. In blistering heat, weary and desperate because of one disaster after another he crouches down in the shade of the car trying to get some shade. At that point:

I catch sight of a man in a red sports car, with the windows up and the air conditioner on, wheeling by. I know exactly who he is: he is a theologian, and he is on his way to the office to write a sermon on the parable of the Good Samaritan – and he's going to pass me by.

This bald summary does no justice to the brilliant way in which the sermon plays with our emotions. The preacher lures us into the story under the guise of explaining how he was preparing the sermon which he has announced he is not going to preach. With him we first view the migrant workers curiously, then empathize with his plight by the side of the road. The moment of truth and the sudden shock of the reversal come without warning and catch us unprepared.

## 6. Use the framework of the parable but change the details

The point of changing details is to reproduce the force of the original, not to produce something better than Jesus. It is the contrast with the original which sharpens the point. Recently I heard Martin Goldsmith work the parable of the Lost Sheep into a sermon. He began the story by counting the sheep in the sheepfold. One, two, three, four, five, six . . . looks of panic flitted across the faces of the congregation. Was he really going to count to 99? But he stopped at six. And then continued in this vein:

> Just six in the fold and 94 out on the mountains. But you have no idea how much time and effort is involved in looking after the pastoral needs of six sheep. It's a major management task. All the feeding and the combing of fleece that is entailed. And then there is the sheepfold. It needs constant repair work and redecoration. Not an easy task. And no one would guess the vast amount of administration involved in looking after six sheep. Meanwhile there are 94 out on the mountains. You may have read a story something like this one in some religious book or other. I just thought I would anglicize the parable for you. Set it in a British context.

It is often said that parables look like simple stories which will be easy to preach. We have seen that, in fact, they bristle with problems. Their very familiarity works against them. Our task is to recapture their original force. In a sermon to the convocation of the clergy preached in 1536 Bishop Hugh Latimer set out a promise which is as relevant to us as it ever was to the first listeners: 'If ye inwardly behold these words, if ye diligently roll them in your minds and afterwards explicate and open them ye shall see our time much touched in these mysteries. Ye shall perceive that God by this example shaketh us by the noses and pulleth us by the ears.'

# PART 3

*The Word embodied in our world*

# 13 Is there life east of Eden?

*Preaching and contemporary culture*

Jesus' sermons connected with the culture of the people. He drew upon
everyday life for his material – a lost coin, the collapse of a tower, a
mugging on a desert road, predicting the weather, a wedding reception. If
culture is the whole life which people live, then preaching which aims to
embody the Word will naturally turn to that life for its examples. A sermon
connects with contemporary culture when the raw material of its content
reflects the life of ordinary people.

*EastEnders*, the long-running BBC soap, has rightly earned the reputation of not being afraid to explore almost every aspect of the human condition. The programme shows that ordinary life is rich in theological
themes. Almost any experience can be mined for the ultimate questions
which it raises. In the same way, films, novels and television dramas take
slices of life and give them a narrative structure. Within these artificial
constraints we can see how an idea or a motif plays in our world, can feel
for ourselves what it's like to be faced with a conflict of values, can think
through an issue or take sides in a debate. Literature and drama present us
with a world view. The programme ends, we switch off the TV and go and
make a cup of tea. It's just a play. But though it may be just a tiny snapshot
of life, through the crafted piece, the author or playwright is making a
claim about the way the world works.

## EVERYONE SHOULD HAVE A SOAP

This would suggest that TV drama, novels and films ought to figure somewhere in the preacher's thinking. In this chapter I shall restrict myself to
TV drama, soaps and quasi-soaps, though most of what I am going to say
is also applicable to films and popular novels. But soaps are viewed by vast
numbers of people. Each week *EastEnders* and *Coronation Street* are
watched by about 12 million viewers every time they are screened, and
*Emmerdale* by around 10 million.[1] Over one-fifth of the population is

watching on any evening. Soaps regularly take the top 14 places in the BBC1 and ITV1 viewing leagues, and even the next positions are taken by quasi-soaps like *Casualty*, *Holby City* and *Midsomer Murders*. This is a phenomenon which should not be ignored or disparaged by the preacher. The Gospels say, 'The common people heard him gladly.' Where did Jesus get the parable of the Dishonest Manager from? Or the Good Samaritan? Or the absentee landlord in the Vineyard parable? Not from the Jewish scriptures. Can preachers afford to be dismissive about any programme which is watched by one-fifth of the population? Soaps, TV and films shape the way people see the world.

I want to use soaps, a term which I take to include long-running series, like *The Bill*, *Casualty*, *Taggart* or *Holby City*, to explore how the preacher might use contemporary culture in preaching. Of course, soaps and TV series are unrealistic. They are exaggerations of real life but can be 'true to life'. In reality, deaths by external causes account for 3.2 per cent of all deaths in the UK but the percentage rises to 64 per cent for soaps. Being an *EastEnders* character is more hazardous than being a Formula One racing driver. Because soaps are working with restricted companies of actors, life crises have to be recycled at breakneck speed. In time, everyone will discover that they are everyone else's mother, long-lost brother, love child, adopted granny. Characters have to express the full range of emotions because every half-hour there has to be a moment of high drama, the cliffhanger which will end the programme. This doesn't always make for subtlety in characterization, but viewers learn the codes. For example, sexual passion is signalled by couples entering a room, shutting the door and immediately tearing the clothes off each other. Anger is depicted as sweeping the items on a desk or table on to the floor. Viewed from the armchair, these actions look slightly ridiculous, a reaction beautifully caught by this preview:

This is the week we say goodbye to Jackie 'careful with that axe'
Owen as she and drug-addled Steve pack those two sets of remarkable Owen eyebrows into a camper van and head for the wide blue
yonder. Jackie had hurled one kitchen implement too many at the
battered Gianni. This week Jackie, her remarkable eyebrows twitching at the sight of a mug tree she just happens to have handy, tells
Gianni that their relationship's over because soon she will have

exhausted her local Habitat's supplies of projectile domestic items. If she doesn't go now it won't be long before she is on the roof of the Vic picking off passers-by with her secret armoury – a 36-piece glazed dinner service with matching coffee pot.[2]

However, although viewers know that soaps massage and exaggerate reality, they still interact with them. The storylines provide role models, personal scripts and an infinite supply of conversation topics. They are stories of people in situations, and their narrative quality makes them fascinating, addictive and self-involving. A producer remarked: 'We don't make life, we reflect it.' This is only partly true, however. Soaps shape society as well as reflect it. When I went onto an Internet search on *East-Enders* I was surprised to find how seriously they were taken by the government, the medical and legal professions and all kinds of pressure groups. Since it started, *EastEnders* has covered homosexuals, rape, unemployment, racism, exams, birth, death, dogs, babies, unmarried mums, teenage pregnancy, prostitution, arranged marriages, attempted suicide, drugs, alcoholism, protection rackets, cot death, extra-marital affairs, urban deprivation, mental breakdown, muggings, suspected murder. Hence the concern that your particular interest should be presented accurately and sympathetically. A newspaper article asks that soaps should show fewer marital break-ups. A medical journal examines how expectations about surgery have been shaped by these programmes. After an episode dealing with pre-menstrual tension, magazines offer information on symptoms or give helpline numbers. Philip Hensher contends, 'Everyone should have a soap opera in their life.'[3] Soaps are not just entertainment.

## THIS IS THE WAY THE WORLD GOES

Soaps communicate a message about 'the way life is'. They don't push this in your face but, all the same, the world of the soap becomes the taken-for-granted world and is accepted without thinking. They help to construct and affirm root paradigms of our society. A root paradigm has been defined as 'an unquestioned and practically unquestionable assumption about the fundamental nature of the world and humanity, underlying and influencing the social actions within a particular cultural context'.[4]

Within this mythological framework ultimate questions of life and death surface – death, suffering, guilt, meaning, the purpose of life, forgiveness, love – together with worked examples of how people cope. Nothing is omitted except politics and swearing.

I used to think that soaps were in practice atheistic, and it is true that they do not present us with a world in which God operates or one in which the church is of any importance. Specifically Christian or church issues are seldom raised. Christians are usually ineffectual stereotypes, judging cake-baking competitions or parroting texts like Dot Cotton in *East-Enders*. But occasionally, a soap will depict a Christian character in a sympathetic or challenging light, and once in a while they will explore faith in a profoundly moving way. Fans of *EastEnders* will remember Dot Cotton's long journey into God-forsakenness. The accurate and moving portrayal of her crisis of faith called forth praise from the Evangelical Alliance.

Television drama has much to teach the preacher. Marsh and Oritz claim: 'Theological discussion is more likely to follow watching a film than listening to a sermon.'[5] That should make us pause. Barbara Tuchman, the historian, is said to keep a warning question in the footer of every page on her computer. It reads, 'Will the reader turn the page?' As far as soaps are concerned, millions do. The same is not always true of sermons. Of course, the material has to be used fast. Tastes change and, in any case, obsolescence is built in. Within a month an incident in a soap will be ancient history, actors leave the casts and reappear in other soaps in a way that can be bewildering until you remember that you saw them last as heroes and now they're villains. By the time you read this book every example will seem quaintly past its sell-by date, like an item in 'That was the year that was.'

## USING THE SOAPS IN SERMONS

The obvious way in which the preacher can tap into the interest in soaps is by using them as *a resource for illustrative material*. They provide us with stock characters and allow off-the-cuff references to well-known types. 'Just like Harold in *Neighbours*' will provoke a nod of recognition from those who watch. They also raise important questions and illustrate dilemmas. A doctor in *Casualty* says to a colleague after a patient had died in horrifying circumstances: 'Pick some meaning out of that.' A poster from the Bible Society campaign in Nottingham posed the question: 'Should Dirty Den's children forgive him for faking his own death?' These are illustrations lying to hand. Of course, to use them effectively implies that the preacher will take the trouble to find out which soaps the congregation is watching.

Here is part of a sermon exploring an incident in *The Vicar of Dibley*:

Unfortunately, Christians are always only half a step away from *Christus domesticus*. We foolishly act as if we are doing him the favour of believing in him and honouring him with our patronage. It would be useful to have Christ at our beck and call, shaped conveniently to our needs. The TV sitcom *The Vicar of Dibley* bought into this notion of the patronized Jesus. The Reverend Geraldine Granger keeps a picture of Christ on the wall and chats away to it (him). He is good to talk to, a little like her simple verger. But when she is about to enter upon a dubious relationship (with an actor last seen playing the part of a consultant in *Casualty*), she turns the portrait to the wall with the words, 'Not your kind of evening.' This is one friend with a mind of his own, however. He is no pushover. Friendship carries obligations. Jesus said, 'You are my friends if you do what I command you' (John 15.14).

Soaps also perform a *legitimizing function*. When they appear in a sermon, they legitimize the preacher, his world and the gospel. The listeners think: 'This preacher lives in our world. He knows about the things we watch.' It was interesting to note how, when *The Matrix* trilogy was first released, references to the films, provided they were accurate, commanded instant attention from student audiences.

The process works in reverse as well. An early review of *A Preaching Workbook* described me as 'an avid TV watcher' and 'a reader of *The Sun*'. (One out of two isn't bad.) In fact, you don't have to watch very much television to stay vaguely in touch with what is going on. The key factor for the preacher is that references to the programmes which the congregation watches, if they are not dismissive or disparaging, legitimize the congregation's culture, viewing habits and taste, and help bridge the gap between the pew and the pulpit.

A third way in which the preacher can constructively use the soaps is by *encouraging critical analysis of the image of Christians and Christianity* which they present. My impression is that programmes are beginning to present Christians in a more rounded fashion. In the past they were usually caricatures – comic figures such as those in *The Vicar of Dibley* and *Father Ted*. But Dot Cotton, whom I suspect is the only chain-smoker in *EastEnders*, has not only become a much-loved character, she has demonstrated love, forgiveness and concern of an attractive kind. Nevertheless, it is still fairly common to see Christians portrayed as intolerant bigots, homophobic and hypocritical. A stock situation will depict a Christian parent who is alienated from his or her child because of a dogmatic and intolerant moral code. Alternatively, Christians are depicted as naïve, slightly weird, out of touch with reality, more likely to pray than do anything useful. In all this, scriptwriters are probably doing no more than reproducing most people's image of Christians. But the preacher can use these stereotypes to open up discussions about what Christians are really like, how much truth there is in the way they are presented and the best way to handle these issues when they arise in conversation outside church.

This consciousness-raising exercise is an aspect of 'equipping the saints' for the apologetics task which faces them at work or at the school gate. There's mileage in exploring the dilemmas of Comfort, the Roman Catholic paramedic in *Casualty*, who has faced moral choices, bereavement and loss of faith, and has related them, admittedly not always constructively, to her faith. The power of the positive image was illustrated in the 2005 New Year's episode of *The Vicar of Dibley*. In a totally unexpected and incredibly moving scene, Geraldine showed her Parochial Church Council video footage of starving African children weeping over the death of their parents. An ordinary sitcom became a cry on behalf of humanity and provoked more than 500 women priests to take a petition to Downing Street.

A fourth way of using soaps in sermons is to take advantage of the fact that they provoke *questions about the nature of existence*. The preacher can grapple with questions such as, 'Is the world really like this? Is it sometimes like this and is this incident true to life? If so, what has the Christian faith to say about it?' Soaps raise ultimate questions. Medical TV dramas are especially good on suffering and the loss of any sense of meaning. In one scene a nurse asks a patient if he is afraid. 'Yes,' he replies. 'I'm frightened to meet God. I don't want to meet someone who gives me AIDS and then adds a fungal infection of the ear.' This image of the Cosmic Sadist cries out for a response from the preacher. By contrast, a nun in a different medical drama watches a cocktail of drugs going into her arm and says, 'I'm wondering how much of God there is in those chemicals.' The doctor replies robustly, 'Fight fire with fire. There's not much of God in the cancer.' By engaging with these incidents the preacher can make a bridge between the contemporary world and the world of the Bible.

Finally, soaps may *provide us with Christ figures*; that is, characters who in some way mirror the grace and generosity of Jesus. Like Babette in *Babette's Feast* they bring richness into people's lives. Perhaps they show forgiveness when wronged or act with integrity or resist temptation. The drama might depict someone transforming a situation by an act of sacrifice or by absorbing hurts. Jesus was happy to use a shepherd, a woman who had lost a coin, a father, a Samaritan, as secular icons of God.

We can take this one step further, rather in the style of the Dilemmas which I described in an earlier chapter. We can insert the person of Christ or Christians into ongoing stories. We can stop the action in the middle of an episode. A preacher can use the sermon to set up the situation and ask, 'What might happen now? What would Christ have done here? What should the Christian do or say?' The sermon can then canvass the possibilities and invite the congregation to continue the dialogue outside the service.

In one sequence of *EastEnders* a couple who had lost their baby agonized over the tragedy. I invited a group to imagine themselves in the situation. 'Let's suppose one or other of the couple came round for a cup of tea. Or you met them at work. What would you *want* to say and do if you were there? What would you bear in mind? And what would you actually say?' I invited people to try out two or three different scenarios. 'Which one is best? Which one is the more Christian? What would have happened if you had gone this way rather than that?' In this way the incident may give us a chance to explore the scandal, the excitement and the liberation of the gospel.

The comments I received after the discussion illustrate the range of reactions:

- The consultant said, 'I know how you feel'. But he didn't and she rightly challenged it.
- He has to own up to the unspoken. She was having to comfort him.
- As a Christian, don't go in like a bull in a china shop.
- Where's the baby now? She wants to know where the baby is now.
- If the baby had been born it would have been born into an unhelpful environment because of all those unresolved issues. There might be healing for them through the miscarriage.
- I would hope they might come to realize that God does love them.
- Lot of Christians feel, 'Why does God allow this?'
- I wouldn't say, 'It's your fault. The two of you should have got married.'
- She wants to talk – it would be better with another woman. The man can't really empathize.
- What about him? He needs healing too – grieving is more difficult for him.
- Crises are often what make people turn to God. It could be the way for them to discover how the tragedy makes sense.
- This happened to me. I wasn't a Christian at the time and I went to a friend for comfort and acceptance because she appeared comforting and accepting. Eventually she gave me a Christian book to read which was really helpful.

This tiny selection of reactions may not strike you as particularly original or earth-shattering. Their value is that they represent people responding to the problem, trying to make their faith and theology concrete.

## A THEOLOGICAL GRID

When dealing with stories taken from contemporary culture it may be helpful to work with a rough checklist of theologically rich concepts. Here is a grid which I have found helpful when trying to plumb the theological possibilities of a novel, a play, a TV drama, a soap or a film. It can be laid over any contemporary drama, film or novel to suggest ways in which the material can be approached. It may expose the implicit religious questions or the 'secular theologies' which lie under the surface.[6]

Does the material deal with the following:

- Questions of absolutes or 'What is reality like?'
- Things which are precious and deemed to be of supreme worth?
- Responses to the natural world – whether use, abuse, stewardship, ecology, conservation, or nature mysticism?
- Experiences of the numinous and related feelings like awe, dread or ecstasy?
- The human predicament – guilt, fear, wrongdoing, fascination with evil, 'the beast' in humanity?
- 'Redemption' or ways of salvation?
- Freedom and choice situations?
- Ideas of good and evil?
- The nature of humanity, whether we are Skinnerian rats, computers, naked apes, or made in the image of God?
- Hope, the future or visions of Utopia?
- Suffering?
- Death and the question of life after death?
- Authority and what is beyond negotiation or dissent?
- Encountering a hero?
- Commitment or 'what I stand for'?
- Protest or 'what I won't stand for'?
- The connection between belief and behaviour?
- Revelation or moments of vision and turning points in life?
- Life maps and the idea of life having a shape?
- The good life?
- Community and living together?
- Rules, laws and commandments; the sense of obligation and 'ought'?
- Love and self-sacrifice?
- Rites of passage, rituals and the expression of beliefs through actions and objects?
- Symbols and icons which point beyond themselves?

This is an amateur attempt to produce a kind of secular theology.[7] Gerd Theissen comments on the 'astonishing analogies in the present secular-ized consciousness, some of which of course can be explained by the fact that the modern world has been persistently shaped by Judaism and

Christianity'.[8] The grid may help us to correlate the doctrines and affirmations of Christianity with the raw experience of people who do not share our belief in God. It may help our congregations to notice and make use of such links in their daily contacts with neighbours, colleagues and friends.

## THE REVERSE ANGLE CAMERA

I end this chapter with an illustration of how engaging with culture was expressed in a specific sermon series. The church which I attend runs an occasional series called Reverse Angle. Those familiar with TV coverage of football will know that the reverse angle camera is the one which shows you what is really going on. It's the one which shows the action which is hidden from the camera that is head on. Adopting this metaphor, the sermon series aims to look at aspects of popular culture from the perspective of Christian faith. In the past three years sermons have covered Harry Potter, *The Simpsons*, Osama Bin Laden, *EastEnders*, *The Matrix*, Mel Gibson's *The Passion of the Christ*, Philip Pullman's *His Dark Materials*, the phenomenon of the Beckhams, the cult of celebrities and Dan Brown's *The Da Vinci Code*.[9]

---

**EXERCISE**

*As a task you might like to use the grid set out above to sketch the outline of a sermon on one of the following topics: any weight-loss regime which is at present appearing in the colour supplements; retail therapy;* Big Brother *or a similar reality TV show; the most recent episode of* East-Enders, Casualty, Emmerdale *or* Coronation Street.

---

When preachers choose to speak on this kind of subject they cannot help making assumptions about the relationship between Christ and the world. Usually these assumptions are left implicit but it is worth spelling them out here. From my perspective, preaching on contemporary culture in the way I have described makes the following affirmations of faith:

- God has not left himself without witness in the culture of today.
- It is worthwhile spending time engaging with it.
- Christians do not have to be contemptuous or disapproving of it.
- The gospel has something vital to say to the whole of life.
- Christians do not have to be terrified or hide in a ghetto.
- Jesus is Lord.

We make the Word concrete by setting it within the culture of our society (which is also the culture of the congregation and the preacher). We try to show that the gospel interacts with the stories and experiences of our world. We tease out its application in our world and trace how Christ relates to the root paradigms of our society. We find analogies for the Word in our world, pointing out in what way it is like this or that feature of secular culture. In any sermon a particular example of today's culture may be commended, resisted, criticized, subverted, or transcended and fulfilled in Christ. But in all this, the rationale of sermons in the style of Reverse Angle echoes Abraham Kuyper's words: 'There's not an inch of secular life of which Christ does not say, "It belongs to me".'

# 14 Picturing the truth

*Preaching and the visual arts*

'After his incarnation icons became an essential way of affirming his appearance in the flesh. To only confess it in word and not in the flesh of material icons, would be a contradiction.'[1] In this way, Brother Aidan makes a plea for using the visual in church. By their nature, pictures make ideas visible. They embody views of the world and make affirmations about life. Do they represent a potential resource for the preacher or do they distract from the clarity of the preached word?

A few years ago a Lent course was published which used Rembrandt's painting of the Return of the Prodigal as its basis. The course included a book of meditations on the painting by Henri Nouwen. It was amazingly successful. Week by week people following the course were moved to deeper insight and very often to tears by the combination of a powerful picture and well-crafted words.

Can the preacher learn from this phenomenon? After I wrote *A Preaching Workbook* I received a helpful letter from a youth leader. She had lots to say about the book and made a number of trenchant comments and helpful suggestions. One remark stuck in my mind, however. She said that, as a youth leader, she had come to the point where she would seldom now speak to teenagers without a visual of some kind.[2] This made me think. Are teenagers so very different from everyone else? Don't we often see a picture which almost seems to demand a comment, a kind of 'sermon in the making'?

The idea that visuals have a role to play in preaching might not be universally accepted. There is a respectable view which believes that using the arts to make a didactic point is to misuse them. Art communicates in its own way. Leave it alone and don't embellish it with chatter. There's a well-known story about Robert Schumann, the composer. Once he played one of his own compositions, and somebody asked him what it meant. Schumann sat down and played it all over again. 'It means that.' You can't reduce art to words. A dance can be described, but it ceases to be a dance.

Lamb's *Tales from Shakespeare* are not Shakespeare. A summary of a poem isn't the poem. Sometimes there's resistance from the preaching side as well. Preaching, it is argued, consists primarily of the exposition of the Bible, this is the preaching of the Word of God. Using a picture as a text is bound to distort the message. The only text allowed is the sacred text of scripture. God has promised to honour that word.

I understand these views but do not share them. Both seem a little doctrinaire. I'm inclined to be more pragmatic. Preaching about pictures may be a crude way of using pictures, but I suspect it has some value. Not every visual used in a sermon is 'great art'. Again, preaching can be true to the gospel without necessarily involving the close exposition of a text. Nevertheless, I freely concede that I am not an expert and that this chapter may border on the impertinent.

## USING VISUALS IN THE SERMON

Plunging in recklessly, I begin by asking what I mean by a visual. Immediately we are struck by the enormous range. Visuals include advertisements, posters, blown-up photos (either works of art, or from magazines and newspapers), one's own photos (here the digital camera is a godsend), Christmas cards, paintings, photos of sculptures, CD sleeves, book covers, one's own large drawings or paintings, stills captured from the television, and all those visuals to be found within the church building itself – a stained-glass window, a banner, stations of the cross, an icon, a cross.

Anything visual may be suitable material for a sermon – either standing on its own or in combination with other visuals, supplementing, complementing or contradicting them, or making up part of a sequence. Even indifferent, bad, mawkish and sentimental pictures can be used to sharpen up a point. A series of sloppy Christmas cards or milk-sop portraits of Jesus allow the preacher to preach in tension with the pictures.

---

**EXERCISE**

*Have you ever used visuals? What did you use? How did you use them? Did you use them in combination with other visuals, and what function did each individual visual play in the total message?*

---

How can we use visuals in a sermon? What can words do when a picture makes its own statement? I offer some ideas without pretending that the following list is exhaustive.

## ATTENDING

Most pictures hope for a reaction. When an artist or a photographer produces a picture or a photograph they are not aiming that it should bore the viewers or leave them unaffected. In fact, they would probably prefer hostility or shock to apathy. Visuals plead for attention. There is a startling painting of the risen Christ which depicts him standing on the ruins of the tomb, with broken columns, statues and armaments in the background. It looks as if Christ's flesh is peeling off his body. He carries an axe and his expression is fearsome. The congregation will see many things in this picture because, code-like, it invites the viewers to decipher the symbolism. This is where words can help. They encourage the congregation to stay longer with the picture than it might naturally be inclined to do. Questions stimulate the act of attending to the picture. They foster deeper perception and provoke keener sight. With many unfamiliar pictures, what is needed is a process of analysis, not in a cold, 'analytical' way but one which nurtures contemplation. Paintings, pictures and photographs make ideas visible. By reason of their framework they exclude and include. Frames determine what is to be seen and what is not in shot. They become statements about the way life is, they sponsor certain values, provoke certain emotions and reactions. The picture is a statement whether we like it or not. And people will read things out of or into a picture. They are reflections on life.

A former colleague, Jennifer Buckham, herself an artist and photographer, suggested that the preacher can help people get to grips with a picture by asking such questions as the following:

- What can you see?
- How has the picture been arranged or organized? What do you notice about its composition?
- What shapes or lines are emphasized? What is centre stage?
- What range of colours has been used?
- What sort of light is there? What's the atmosphere of the picture?

- What do you notice about the figures which are not in the limelight? What do you notice about the background? Does the picture illustrate a story?
- Do you think the artist is conveying a message?
- What effect does the painting have on you?

Words can help people to be attentive to the picture. They can encourage them to notice details, the expressions and stances of figures, the effect of tone and colours and what may appear to be incidentals like the background. I once used Rembrandt's picture of the Good Samaritan arriving at the inn. Right in the forefront a dog crouches, doing what dogs do naturally. The congregation noticed the dog but was not sure what it was to do with it. I offered the suggestion that Rembrandt was trying to say that works of mercy have to be performed in this messy world, where we go about our business and so do dogs.

The importance of attending was brought home to me when I heard a lecture entitled 'Where did Christ die, iconographically speaking?' Though the title was not immediately appealing, the lecture was riveting. It examined the background and location of crucifixion paintings and what they said about the meaning of the death of Christ. Grunewald's Christ is crucified near to the ground against what looks like a nuclear wasteland, the aftermath of Hiroshima. Salvador Dali's Christ is spread-eagled against outer space. Another artist sets Christ in the tranquillity of the countryside, with sober and pious peasants kneeling round as if the Angelus had just sounded. Each background adds something to the meaning of the painting and invites a different understanding of the atonement. What I found interesting was that the words did not denude the pictures of their emotional force; they enhanced it.

## ARTICULATING

The commonest way in which words relate to pictures is as a commentary. Here the preacher is trying to reflect on the message of the picture and bring out an understanding of its meaning. When I have been on the receiving end of this I have often had the odd experience of suddenly seeing something about life or the gospel or the nature of God which I had long suspected was there but hadn't been able to put into words. The reflective commentary highlights and explains what I am looking at but extends its reference so that it becomes a true sermon, making personally relevant what began as something external and detached. Nouwen's meditations on the Prodigal fall into this category. So did the tape commentary on the paintings in the National Gallery's 'Seeing Salvation' exhibition. I think of a sermon on a rose window which reflected on the shape of a circle as an image of time and eternity, on the implications of Christ at its centre and the throng of creatures, both angelic and human, who surrounded him.

> Some of the figures in the outer circle have two stars by their heads, some have one, some have no stars at all. I have no idea why. And it doesn't seem to bother them. I suspect that down here there would be a General Synod paper on 'The random distribution of astral bodies: an equal opportunities issue'. The centre of the rose unites the various points on the circumference. We speak of people being diametrically opposed. But in the window we cannot imagine people who are diametrically opposed cat-calling or backbiting across the circle. For their words have to pass through the figure of Christ. Here, there can be no cheap slogans designed to do others down: happy clappy evangelicals; moany groany Anglo-Catholics, wishy-washy liberals. For Christ is at the centre. The barbs will have to pass through his body in order to strike their target.

The advantage of preaching on something like a rose window is that the image will remain in the mind and will still be there next Sunday.

But whatever the image, it will make a statement about the nature of the world. In this sense all pictures are icons, windows into reality. As still pictures they lend themselves to elucidation and exposition. I remember a photograph which took the form of a cross about four feet high by three feet wide and which consisted of a close-up of the graffiti sprayed and carved into the stone work of an ancient church. Most of the graffiti looked as if it came from teenagers. The photo set up an interesting tension and was a powerful statement of something which couldn't quite be put into words. It cried out for a preacher to articulate its message.

*Imagine this photo. If you had to give a ten-minute reflection on the images, what direction would you take?*

Perhaps you took the line that the photo was about the church. Is it saying that the church is in decay, scorned and defaced by those who lived around it? Maybe you decided that the image was about the body of Christ as the place where the world carves its rejection of God. Perhaps it was a statement about Christ's vulnerability and his willingness to absorb the pain of the world. Some of those who saw the photo picked up the sense of despair and aimlessness in the graffiti, arguing that they pointed to young people lost in an inner-city wilderness.

I think there are advantages in restricting yourself to still pictures. Recently I have seen preachers making use of film clips in sermons. At first this seemed one step up from the still frame, but now I'm less sure. One disadvantage with the clip is that it brings with it a load of uncontrollable baggage. With a still you can set the context briefly, giving only as much background information as is needed for the purposes of the sermon. You also freeze the action at the very moment you want. If the clip is from a film that is well known then there may be yet more seepage as the listeners bring attitudes which are already formed. Many of the problems we associate with the use of lengthy story illustrations are similar to those encountered when film clips are used.

## ACCOMPANYING

Words can work alongside pictures. A poem read while a particular visual is on the screen is not so much a commentary on the picture as an accompaniment to it. Poem and picture work together to produce an effect. In this category I would include the prayer which invites the congregation to keep its eyes open while the images scroll through. Like instruments in an orchestral piece or singer and accompanist, words and visuals interact. Just as a caption can change the way you 'read' a picture, so the words help you respond to the image in a certain way. But equally, the emotions engendered by the picture feed back into the words.

From years ago, I remember a black and white poster from the United Society for the Propagation of the Gospel. It depicted an African woman, heavily pregnant, walking gracefully across a narrow bridge. The meditation which accompanies this image contained these lines:

> One day I will be outside;
> I will look at her; she will remember
> And I will be in tune with her remembering.
> Her anxieties will be mine,
> And perhaps I will know where they came from.
> My maker knows this process;
> He too has been inside
> And has broken out.
> 'When you became man to set us free
> you did not abhor the virgin's womb.'
> God has chosen to be part of his world,
> To be right inside what he has made.[3]

---

**EXERCISE**

*What words would you choose to accompany the picture of Edvard Munch's 'The Scream'? You are not attempting a commentary here. Is there a poem or a prayer which will work with the picture? Can you think of a biblical passage which might fit? Is there a second picture which might set up a tension with Munch's painting?*

---

ENGAGING

Preachers can try to encourage active engagement with a visual. Now their aim is to get the congregation to do things with the picture – not just understand it better but enter it, pummel it, knead it, and let it pummel and knead them in its turn. The words become an invitation to a conversation. If every picture tells a story, then questions like these compel the congregation to engage with the action: What has just happened? What will happen next? What are they all thinking? What are their hopes and dreams? What is this particular person thinking? What questions would you like to ask the person in the picture? How will it all end? How would you like it to end? I'm not suggesting that the sermon consist entirely of questions. The sermon form means that most of the questions are both asked and answered by the preacher. But interrogating the congregation and encouraging active thought involves the listeners in the world of the picture.

For example, there is a Rembrandt cartoon which shows Jesus walking on the water. Peter has got out of the boat but is sinking fast and, at the point that Rembrandt has frozen the scene, he is up to his neck. His face shows absolute terror. Jesus leans forward to raise him up. But back at the boat a second figure has climbed over the side and is caught with one foot about to touch the water and two hands behind his back firmly gripping the side of the boat. (This may be a sketch of Peter at an earlier stage in the story, but forget that possibility for now.) Yet another figure leans out, observing what is going on.

This picture is wonderfully rich material for the preacher. There is plenty for analysis – the gesture of Jesus, the expression of Peter, the posture of the second disciple – but it allows for engagement as well. Ask people what each character is thinking or saying and you receive a wide variety of reactions. Is Peter thinking 'What a fool I was' or 'Well, at least I tried'? Is the second disciple regretting the bold move which took him outside the boat or kicking himself for his reluctance to go the whole way and let go? Is the observer wistful and longing to be with the others or thinking smugly, 'You didn't oughta done that'? But this range of responses mirrors our own reactions when we feel Christ calling us to dare great things for his sake and gives us an outline structure for the sermon.

## INVOLVING

This is one stage on from engaging. Here the preacher invites people into the picture, to become one of the actors or to be themselves within the story. Many Good Friday meditations have concentrated on the figures standing at the foot of the cross and have tried to enter their thoughts. Sometimes the preacher has asked listeners to stand at the cross in their own persona and watch as Christ suffers for them. Personal involvement in a scene can be a profound experience. Which character am I? If I am in the picture, what am I doing and saying? Where does this touch me? How am I feeling? If I am myself, what am I feeling and doing? What is Christ saying to me?

Here is Thomas Troeger combining engaging and involving in a sermon on Rembrandt's painting of Joseph and Mary asleep by the manger.[4]

> Mary is a round faced peasant woman
> Leaning up against the manger
> Her eyelids
> Closed.
> The shadow on her face suggests
> A new mother whose energy
> Is sapped
> By immediate demands
> And future fears.
> Her left arm is slouched around the child on the hay.

So far the preacher is taking the congregation through the painting, adding his own imaginative commentary. Later on he steps into the picture.

> I call out:
> 'Mary,
> Joseph,
> Wake up!
> Didn't you hear the angel?
> I know you are tired.
> You have every reason to be.
> But the salvation of the world
> Is depending on you.
> If you don't act,
> God's newborn love won't have a chance.'

And then Troeger makes his main point.

> Then I become still,
> Shocked by my own words . . .
> Would God be foolish enough
> To let heaven's purpose hang
> On such a fragile human link –
> As fragile as Mary slouched around the manger?

# 15 Powerful or pointless?

*Preaching with PowerPoint*

I remember the man who sold me my computer. At the point at which he handed it over, his voice deepened and became heavy with awe and wonder. 'It's got PowerPoint on it,' he intoned, 'Very powerful tool for presentations.' At the time I was deeply impressed, though he might as well have been speaking about the cloak of invisibility or the elixir of life. Years later, most people know about PowerPoint, and a PowerPoint industry has mushroomed.

Embodying the Word naturally involves using pictures, because pictures capture ideas and present them visually. PowerPoint is a tool designed precisely to do this, and it does it in a reliable, high-quality, user-friendly way. As a consequence, sermons are increasingly making use of PowerPoint. The Internet reveals hundreds of sites devoted entirely to PowerPoint presentations. For a relatively modest outlay you can have your next 50 sermons ready to go and captured on a CD. Slogans like 'There's PowerPoint in the blood' and 'PowerFul Preaching' present PowerPoint as an indispensable tool.

At the same time not everyone is equally impressed. Edward Tufte wrote a seminal essay criticizing what PowerPoint does to the way we think.[1] He is credited with saying, 'Power corrupts. And PowerPoint corrupts absolutely.' Others have argued that it's 'more Power than Point' or spoken of 'death by PowerPoint', 'bullet-point coma' and 'Powerpointlessness'. 'PowerPoint poisoning' and 'mind candy' are other examples of a widespread suspicion of the package. My personal favourite is 'Killing me Microsoftly . . .'.

It is true that it is difficult to condense carefully crafted, image-laden phrases into short, bullet-point headings. Peter Norvig famously debunked PowerPoint with a jokey presentation of the Gettysburg Address and was amazed to find that it rang bells with hundreds of people. It begins in a way all too familiar with those of us who have sat through PowerPoint presentations:

And now please welcome President Abraham Lincoln.

Good morning. Just a second while I get this connection to work. Do I press this button here? Function-F7? No, that's not right. Hmmm. Maybe I'll have to reboot. Hold on a minute. Um, my name is Abe Lincoln and I'm your president. While we're waiting, I want to thank Judge David Wills, chairman of the committee supervising the dedication of the Gettysburg cemetery. It's great to be here, Dave, and you and the committee are doing a great job. Gee, sometimes this new technology does have glitches, but we couldn't live without it, could we? Oh – is it ready? OK, here we go.

Lincoln spoke these resonant lines:

We are met on a great battlefield of that war. We have come to dedicate a portion of that field as a final resting-place for those who here gave their lives that that nation might live. It is altogether fitting and proper that we should do this. But in a larger sense, we cannot dedicate, we cannot consecrate, we cannot hallow this ground.

In the spoof presentation they appear as:

Things we aren't going to do:
- Dedicate
- Consecrate
- Hallow.

Of course, the preacher isn't in the same situation as the executive trying to make a pitch and clinch a deal. It is still worth asking how PowerPoint can play the part of a tool and not become a master. Does PowerPoint have advantages built in and can we note disadvantages which we need to guard against?

## BUILT-IN ADVANTAGES

1  PowerPoint is the best tool so far designed for projecting bright, sharp, high quality pictures. It is light years ahead of other methods. If you

remember making your own large-scale pictures and diagrams (though they were probably not much larger than A3 size) or trying to draw them on to OHP acetate sheets or holding them up (a nightmare for the biceps) or, worse still, hoping the congregation could see the photograph in the book you were holding, then the superiority of PowerPoint hardly needs to be argued. A picture can be scanned into a presentation within minutes. It is possible to take a digital photograph at the beginning of a service and have it inserted into the presentation before the end of the first hymn. PowerPoint produces high quality, colourful, large pictures (in the region of eight feet by six if those are the proportions you need). Computer techies may mutter that PowerPoint is not the best projection software around, just the best promoted; but as a complete non-specialist, I am not aware of anything to equal it at the moment.[2]

2   PowerPoint works with the visual. Pictures on a screen grab the attention of the congregation. They support and clarify the spoken word and help to fix ideas in the memory. Pictures can sometimes speak more eloquently than words. The old aphorisms, 'One picture is worth a thousand words' and 'One in the eye is worth two in the ear' ring true. Every slide re-engages the congregation. Even those who are thoroughly bored still look up when the screen changes.

3   A third built-in advantage is PowerPoint's capacity to lock music onto words and images. This makes it a trouble-free resource for those preparing visual reflections and meditations or leading the congregation into prayer.

## BUILT IN-DISADVANTAGES

1   PowerPoint has its disadvantages as well. A friend wrote to me with a warning: 'Get hooked on what PowerPoint can do and it adds hours to your preparation time. The key question I have to keep asking myself is: Is the gimmick enhancing or distracting from the communication? And because I like playing with toys, I find it difficult to keep it simple.' If a set of slides is sitting in the laptop we can be sure that the preacher hasn't just jotted a few idle thoughts on the back of an envelope, but producing those slides will have added around three hours to the preparation time.

2   The very power of the visual also constitutes its greatest danger for the preacher. In a battle between a preacher, however photogenic, and a large luminous object, the preacher will lose eight times out of ten. If you do not take steps to ensure that you stay in control the PowerPoint screen will take over. You are then left with the task of getting people back. In fact, I have noticed that I will look at a screen even when there's nothing on it, waiting patiently for it to start twinkling again. To make matters worse, the screen has to be positioned to the side of or behind you. Eye contact is lost, it's hard for people to watch body language or listen carefully when something brighter and more colourful is going on in the wings.

## HOW CAN THE PREACHER STAY IN CONTROL?

The key for the preacher then is staying in control and ensuring that programs such as PowerPoint are a servant and not a master. Maybe we need to bear in mind some basic ground rules.

### Eliminate distractions
*Visibility*
Can people at the sides see the screen or is the preacher in the way? Are there side aisles which block sight lines?

*Timing*
It is very important that a point does not come up on screen before you have finished the previous one. Ideally you want the punch-lines to come up as you speak. This probably means that you will have to control the slide changes yourself, and have a laptop screen facing you so that you see what is happening without having to turn round and check on the big screen. Unfortunately this may impede your natural preaching style, and the laptop with associated spaghetti can itself be an irritation. One member of the congregation said to me: 'I don't like worshipping the graven image of a data projector. It doesn't do anything for the sense of the numinous.' As an alternative, you could rehearse the whole sermon with a stooge, but this is very time-consuming and stressful for the stooge.

*Transitions*

Slide changes which come zipping in from left, right, top and bottom, or explode on the screen, often with the sound of shattering glass or screeching tyres, are gimmicks and become intensely irritating in a very short time. 'Don't dazzle!' is sound advice.

*Formats*

In the same way, slides which use every font, pitch and colour in the pack draw attention to the appearance of the slide and away from its content. A single font or at most two (perhaps one for headings and another for quotations) carried consistently through the presentation are likely to be less distracting.

## Choose your words

What is the function of the words on the screen? And how will they work best?

First, most sermons have a teaching content and it may help to fix that in the listeners' minds if the heading appears on the screen. The ideal is a crisp, clear, large-print statement which captures and summarizes the idea. The commonest mistake is to crowd the screen with words. Paragraph headings in newspapers are often used merely to break up blocks of text; they do not indicate moves in the logical structure of the argument. In a sermon, bullet points which just break up material or fill the screen will confuse rather than clarify.

Second, carefully crafted words designed to move people, to touch hearts, draw people into a story or change a way of looking at the world will work better when spoken than when reduced to bullet points. Words which clarify and summarize are obviously helpful at some point in a sermon, but headings are not the best instrument for stirring emotions. 'How to' sermons hammer their points home, and major on exhortation and advice. The excerpt from the Gettysburg Address illustrates how banal the PowerPoint words are compared with Lincoln's prose. Trust the preaching of the Word and the passion of the preacher.

Third, words on a screen work well when presenting brief quotations. Quotations, either from the Bible or some other source, are notoriously difficult to listen to. Part of the problem is that anything but the very shortest quotation will disappear from consciousness. However, text on a screen remains for as long as you want it and it allows the congregation to scan it, going back and picking up what was missed the first time round. Biblical quotations can focus on a key phrase or a word by highlighting. The text can be revealed gradually as the preacher expounds first one part and then another. The reverse technique may work as well. The full verse appears on the screen, but as you read it the words disappear. When you have finished reading there are just one or two words left on the screen, and those are the key words from the paragraph.

A fourth way of using words is to make the screen a partner in the dialogue. The screen can comment on what you are saying. For example, at one point in a sermon on 'Time' the preacher was talking about time management courses and suggesting that it is much more difficult to get a grip on time than these courses often suggest. 'You know the kind of advice they give . . .' At this point the screen read as follows, each bullet point appearing in turn:

- Identify priorities.
- Don't let the urgent overwhelm the important.
- Work smarter, not longer.
- Clear your desk!
- Learn to say no or you will become the servant of other people's priorities.

The preacher commented: 'These are all useful ideas but they're very difficult to put into practice. So sometimes we add two of our own . . .' He stopped speaking but on the screen appeared:

- Burn the handouts.
- Kill the lecturer.

A similar technique is to use the screen to comment on what you're saying – like 'thinks bubbles'. This can be negative ('What rubbish!', 'If you believe that, you'll believe anything') or more constructive ('Haven't you left God out of the picture?', 'Why not try praying?').

Again, you can leave headings, summaries or questions on the screen at the end of the sermon as an after-image. They can become ways into prayer, confession or reflection. These strategies all help in making words our servants and not our masters.

Finally, there seems to be a consensus on what not to do with words. One experienced PowerPoint operator has put it this way: 'There's a not uncommon practice of turning your back on the audience and reading aloud what they are reading already. This is an absolute no-no. Can we have zero tolerance on reading out what the screen says?'[3]

## Know your pictures

The key to staying in control when using pictures is to have decided in advance what you want each picture to do. Not every image performs the same function. We might categorize pictures under these headings.

*Pictures as information*
Maps, graphs, diary entries, timelines, dates and survey findings come under this heading.

*Pictures as icons*
Under this heading I would include all those images whose purpose is primarily to convey a mood. Of course they will give information; it's very hard for a picture not to do so. However, a slide of a storm may have little to do with the weather forecast but say a lot about the threat of disaster. A photograph of a still figure in a garden may yield information about flowers and shrubs but its main purpose will be to suggest stillness, contemplation and prayer. A thorn on the branch of a rose is probably less about horticulture than the passion of Christ.

*Pictures as association points*
Pictures which are iconic work as metaphors, pointing beyond themselves. In a related category I would place those images which are stereotypes and clichés – shorthand visual language. A nurse at a bedside says 'Caring', a teenager on a station platform says 'Leaving home'. A test tube with a Bible may point to science and religion. A clock showing a minute to midnight says 'Last chance'. Stereotypes and visual clichés are useful for making an instant connection with an idea. Associations come attached to the picture. Of course there are visual clichés which are not much more than eye candy. A lot of clip art falls into this category. Do we

really need that cartoon of a man with a light bulb over his head to suggest revelation?

*Pictures as analogies*
Sometimes the picture is a visual analogy. I remember seeing a clip from an international rugby match which introduced the idea of teamwork in church leadership. Such images need to be handled with care. They run the same risk of 'seepage' as verbal analogies. It is true that there is some common ground between the community of the church and a rugby team, but the visual is so overwhelmingly powerful that the slender connection can get submerged. In the same way a photo of a law court won't say much about the doctrine of justification.

*Pictures as puzzles*
Just occasionally a picture will function mainly as a puzzle. It invites the viewer to decipher what is going on or what it means. I remember a freeze-frame from the TV programme *Price Drop TV*. On the screen was a man selling a gourmet set of saucepans, a notice board showing the original price of the items, another board showing how the price was falling minute by minute and a third board showing how many sets were left. Along the bottom of the picture ran a line of names and addresses of those who had already purchased saucepans. All the time the clock was counting down the time that was left. There was an incredible amount of detail in the picture and it invited the congregation to observe, decipher and react to what was going on. In case you wonder what on earth such an image was doing in a sermon, it was an elaborate way of illustrating Paul's injunction: 'Grab each moment as it comes past' or 'redeeming the time' (Colossians 4.5).

*Pictures as stories*
Some pictures freeze a moment within a continuing story and I have dealt with these in the preceding chapter. They invite conversation and commentary and the preacher may want to respond to them in a variety of ways – analysing, articulating the message, accompanying the image with poetry or a Bible reading, or helping the congregation to engage or get personally involved.

This rough categorization is trying to demonstrate the value of knowing what kind of a picture you are showing and what you want it to do. Puzzle pictures cry out for a pause in the sermon while people engage with them. Icons and stereotypes do their job best if left alone. Story pictures need the preacher to speak about or with them. Many pictures can operate under more than one heading, but all pictures need to be controlled by the plotline of the sermon.

Pictures are both powerful and full of problems. Because they are specific they can narrow down an idea to a particular image of it, so that 'authority and power' ends up as a photograph of Tony Blair. They are not good at representing motives or thoughts. Visualizing an abstract concept can distort or trivialize it. A medieval mosaic of Jesus riding into Jerusalem on a donkey sets the event in a distant time and place. Most preachers will feel 'I can do better with my eyes, my hands, my face and my voice.' We know, of course, that there are some things that pictures do superbly well. The moral seems to be 'Choose pictures carefully. Don't use too many. And don't expect the software to speak for you. It won't.'

## FREE THE SPIRIT

A sermon is not a lecture, and the danger of using slides is that we can speak to them as in a lecture. 'Use the slides and don't let them use you' sounds good advice, but how is it to be put into practice?

Ian Parker tells an encouraging story of a Microsoft executive:

> Jolene Rocchio, who is a product planner for Microsoft Office . . . argued against a speaker's using PowerPoint at a future conference. I said, 'I think we just need her to get up and speak.' On an earlier occasion, Rocchio said, the same speaker had tried to use Power-Point and the projector didn't work, 'and everybody was, like, cheering. They just wanted to hear this woman speak, and they wanted it to be from her heart. And the PowerPoint almost alienated her audience.'[4]

'They wanted it to be from her heart.' The first point then is to trust the spoken word and the passion that is expressed by the preacher who has prayed him- or herself hot and is speaking in the freedom that the Spirit gives. Alongside that trust I would emphasize the importance of keeping the argument or plot of the sermon in view at every stage, from preparing the slides to delivering the sermon. PowerPoint does things to preachers and the temptation to put in a picture because you've got it or a set of bullet points because you can is always at hand. There's more than one way of jumping off the pinnacle of the temple. But the plot of the sermon will tell you if that visual or that summary is necessary or just a diversion.

A second threat to the Spirit is that preachers can feel locked into the presentation. The text is preplanned and stuck in predestined grooves. There seems to be no way you can short cut or digress until you reach the terminus. This problem is well nigh insuperable if someone else is running the slides for you, short of giving them public instructions. But in any case it's not good to feel that you have effectively restricted the Spirit's sovereignty.

All is not lost. You can jump slides if time is slipping by. Type in a slide number and hit RETURN and you will be taken forward to that particular slide without the others showing. Similarly, you can blank the screen. If you hit B the screen will go Black and if you hit W, the screen will go White. Hitting B or W again brings the screen back at the point where you left it. This allows you to make the screen disappear for a while and hold attention in your own right.

How can you stop turning into a narrator or commentator on pictures, a kind of voice-over in a TV documentary? I have already argued that you cannot compete with the flashing lights in the corner. The screen turns heads and you lose eye contact – one of the most precious tools you have. At its worst the screen will inhibit you – making gestures redundant. You need to get the congregation back so that vivid imagery, word play and illuminating images can do their work. The PowerPoint is not preaching the sermon. It would be terrible if this tool limited your gifts.

This is where the recurring slide comes in. You can 'give permission' to the congregation to look at a slide by cueing it in ('Look at this picture by Rembrandt') and then when you have finished using the picture, you draw attention back by changing the slide to something that is not novel, for example a background that has been a leitmotif or a list of the main headings at the point where you last left it.

So what do you think? Are you a PowerPoint junkie? Or are you determined to avoid the big screen at all costs? Maybe you are just ready to give it a hesitant go. I suggest that PowerPoint, like marriage, is 'not to be taken in hand, unadvisedly, lightly or wantonly, to satisfy carnal lusts and appetites, like brute beasts that have no understanding'. On the other hand, think carefully about a call to absolute celibacy.

# 16 Handling the invisible

*Preaching with objects*

I heard a true story about a young minister arriving early to church and starting to prepare everything he needed for the service. Since he was due to preach, he took a large hammer and some seven-inch nails out of a bag and placed them near the pulpit. A senior steward had also arrived early. 'What have you got those for?' he asked. 'It's not an All Age, is it?' There is a strange idea that using objects in sermons ought to be reserved for children's addresses.

No book on embodying the Word can omit preaching with objects. Think back to those occasions when you have seen them used in an address. Sometimes, no doubt, you squirmed with embarrassment when far-fetched connections were being made between an everyday object and a theological idea. Occasionally, perhaps, you watched in consternation as the Lego tower collapsed. I heard a story about a Christmas Day address which involved a mystery parcel. 'Now,' said the preacher, 'I've got a present here, all wrapped up in this shiny paper.' Then more conspiratorially, 'And I wonder what it can be.' The friend who told me this story swears that a little girl put up her hand and said 'It's a present. It's free. It's the baby Jesus. And it's for all of us.' When that happens there's not much you can do except sing a hymn.

Such stories may discourage us from using objects in sermons. But there will be other memories – of times when the object fixed the truth so firmly in our minds that years later we can still remember what it symbolized. I once heard a talk 'Taking everything to God in prayer'. The speaker suddenly picked up her handbag and started to take out the contents one by one, putting them on the table in front of her. 'This is how we come to God,' she said, 'We take each little bit of our lives and lay them in front of him.' We were impressed. But then she started to collect up the bric-a-brac. 'The trouble is, when we've done that,' she went on, 'we pick up all the worries and problems, put them back in the bag again and carry them away with us.' I've been surprised how often that image has returned to mind.

The question for me then is not whether I should ever use objects with adult congregations but how I can use them most effectively.


## 1. THE OBJECT AS ITSELF

I begin at the most obvious point. Objects do not always have to represent something else. They can communicate just by being themselves. For example, Robert Pagliari suggests that if you are going to refer to an event in the newspaper then a more dynamic and engaging way of doing so is by holding up the paper and apparently reading the excerpt from it.[1]

He draws attention to the range of objects in the church – 'wafers, wine, water, candles, pews, font, stations, Easter candles, collection plates, pillars, windows, lights, instruments, hymnals, flowers, carpets, colours, textures, the pulpit itself' – and asks, 'When was the last time you pointed to the altar, the cross or the Bible when you were giving a sermon?'[2]

His thesis seems to be that the more sensory experiences you can build into the sermon, the more it is likely to stay in the memory of the congregations. People who come to church are viewers as well as listeners.

Referring to any artefact will direct and hold attention to some extent but an object will give up more of its significance if it is handled and if the preacher tells its story. I remember an elderly member of a church using his Bible in an address. He held it up. It was well thumbed and looked rather shabby. But he described it as one of the most precious things he owned. He told us about one or two critical experiences in his life and described how the Bible had helped him. As we watched the reverent way in which he held it and turned the pages, we were receiving an eloquent message. He was not offering us extra information about the book but communicating its preciousness.

On another occasion, a teacher spoke about a pen which a class had given him. The class began the year as the students from hell and represented one of the most troublesome groups he'd ever had to teach. But he persisted and, rather to his surprise, they gave him the pen at the end of the school year. He described how one of the worst offenders acted as spokesman. He handed over the package, slightly embarrassed. 'Here y'a, sir', he said, 'We got you a present.'

## 2. THE OBJECT AS QUESTION

Objects can play a different role. An unfamiliar object in a familiar context will raise a question: What's that doing there? I remember bringing a packet of washing powder into the pulpit only to find that a zealous worshipper had removed it before the service began. If the object is in full view but left without comment it will naturally create suspense and maintain attention. Everyone will expect you to resolve the tension soon and curiosity will keep them watching.

Dave McClellan gives three examples from his own preaching. When he wanted to speak about suffering he calculated that a wooden cross was too familiar an object for his audience. So he brought in an intravenous bag suspended from its holder. He says that for another occasion 'I started a sermon with a battered, old chair to the left of the pulpit. It was there throughout the worship, leaving people to wonder who forgot to take out the trash. But when it came time to preach on God's passion for restoring broken-down lives, I had the visual cue right beside me. The tension, which had been building since I started, was released.' Another time he put a Styrofoam cup and a hand-crafted ceramic mug on top of the pulpit and left them there for most of the sermon without comment. It was only at the end, when he came to speak about the lasting value of God's individual workmanship, that he contrasted the two mugs.[3] I remember a preacher planting a broken clock in full view of the congregation without comment. Later he spoke about ineffective ways of trying to get it to work again and the need for a new set of works inside.

But the most memorable example of suspense created by using an object came during a sermon delivered to a largely academic congregation. The preacher was joined by a snake, a glove puppet which she had concealed in the sleeve of her academic gown. Sidney, for such was its name, joined her in the sermon, following the text carefully, whispering in the preacher's ear and staring unabashed at the congregation. I don't think

I took my eyes off that snake. And, before you challenge me, I do remember both the passage and the sermon, but I'm not going to go into detail. You had to have been there.

Finally, I wonder what you make of this example. A friend writes of hearing a famous speaker preaching about global mission. He says, 'The whole time he preached he was bouncing an inflatable globe up and down! He said nothing about it but it reinforced his message.' Again, perhaps you had to have been there.


## 3. THE OBJECT AS TRIGGER

Objects carry associations with them so that every time you encounter them, they evoke memories. Preachers hope to tie the meaning into the object so that their listeners will be unable to remember one without the other. Celtic spirituality links putting on your clothes with breastplate prayers – 'I bind unto myself this day the strong name of the Trinity.' Having a shower or a bath may pull in memories of baptism or cleansing. Pouring water from a jug may trigger a memory of a sermon where this was used to represent the grace of God poured out in love on us. A stone may remind you of the resurrection.

I heard a sermon where the preacher told the story of Elisha and the widow's jar of oil (2 Kings 4.1–7). Elisha commanded the woman, 'Go outside, borrow vessels from all your neighbours, empty vessels and not just a few.' In the story she did so and in the sermon suddenly the whole platform area around the preacher was covered in jars, basins, jugs and saucepans (with, as I remember it, one colander!). The preacher made the point that the oil went on flowing while there were receptacles to contain it. He said, 'And the message is: bring out all the jars you've got and God will fill them. More jars, more blessing.'[4] How many people who were there will recall that word every time they open their kitchen cupboards?

We can see the principle of association at work when we consider the example of Jesus. As the disciples argue about pre-eminence, he takes 'a little child and puts it by his side'. He says, 'Whoever welcomes this child in my name, welcomes me' (Luke 9.48). Answering a double-edged question about paying tribute to Caesar, he asks for a coin and displays the image and superscription on it (Matthew 22.19–20). The object makes the idea present and does so in three-dimensional, tactile form. It binds itself tightly to the truth it embodies so that later on, seeing or handling a coin will pull the message with it, just as the smell of wood smoke can take you back in memory 20 years to an autumn afternoon. Could broken bread and wine poured into a cup ever be the same for the disciples after the upper room? Would a towel and a basin of water ever again be just ordinary, household items? I doubt it. Jesus had filled them with meaning.

## 4. THE OBJECT AS ICON

It is evening. In the semi-darkness a group of Christians stand holding lighted candles. They look into the flame. The leader of worship invites them to see the flame as pointing to the mystery of God, to see in it an icon of his infinity and the eternal movement that cannot be contained. She speaks of a light in the darkness, draws attention to its weakness and vulnerability but also to the illumination it gives and the way the brightness is reflected off the faces of those who gaze into it. One of the most powerful ways in which objects can be used is as analogies or icons, pointing to an invisible truth.

It may be a powerful way but it is also fraught with problems. Anything can be used as an analogy of anything else. If the connection is obscure, contrived or trivial, it may work against effective communication. Life is indeed like a sardine tin and there probably is always a little bit tucked away on the side, but we need to remember that Alan Bennett concocted that analogy when he wanted to *parody* a sermon.

There's a telling illustration of the double-edged nature of object-analogies in one of Cathy Fox's novels. Mara, the main character, is in a tutor's study and notices a hyacinth bulb. The tutor recalls a Sunday School teacher who told her when she was a child that it was an illustration of the resurrection.

'You took me right back to my childhood,' said Dr Roe. 'If only you knew how many things were supposed to remind me of the Lord Jesus. Pepper pots, weather vanes, soap bubbles . . .'

'Shoes with reinforced metal toes,' said Mara. It was out before she could stop it.

'Exactly. And I cannot remember in one single case,' said Dr Roe, 'why they were supposed to remind me of Jesus.'[5]

Over the last 30 years I've read a number of reports of preachers eating daffodils in the pulpit on Easter morning. I've never been quite sure how this analogy works but perhaps it goes something like this: 'I've just eaten a daffodil. That's such a strange thing to have done that if you went and told someone who wasn't here they would never believe you. But it happened just the same. And you can tell them that it happened. It's just like that with the resurrection. It was such a strange thing that no one would believe it. Except that it really did happen. And we know that it did, because the disciples said they'd seen it with their own eyes.' This seems to me a convoluted parallel. The preacher would be better finding a different analogy, not least because a number of those who have eaten daffodils have ended up in hospital.

Another analogy likens the character of the disciple to the ingredients of a cake. The ingredients are brought out and mixed in front of the congregation. Real ingredients are used (flour, sugar and so on) but the commentary describes them as three pounds of love, a pinch of humour, half a pound of patience, etc. Eventually 'one I made earlier' is produced. I think the weakness of this analogy lies in its contrived nature. There is no obvious connection between flour and sugar and humour and patience.

By contrast, consider the use of objects in this All Age address. The preacher tells the story of Mother's birthday. The children get up early and decide to make her breakfast. Everything goes wrong. The porridge is burnt, the toast is black, the tea is cold, the tray is awash with milk, by mistake they use salt instead of sugar. But it's the best the children can manage. When they take it upstairs to mum, she doesn't scold them for making a mess. She's touched by their efforts and really appreciates what they have tried to do for her. What I like about this story is that the objects all play themselves; there's no tortuous allegory involved. When the preacher says, 'And God's like that with our efforts to please him', the analogy is carried by the overall structure of the story.[6]

It is not easy to get object-analogies right. I watched a news item which showed Andrew Marr, the BBC's political correspondent, throwing darts at a board in order to illustrate the ideas of government targets. It seemed slightly patronizing. On the other hand I can see it working as an illustration of the root idea of sin as 'missing the mark'.

Here are two examples of object-analogies which made a lasting impression on those who heard and saw them. The first concerns an address by Helen Roseveare who had been captured by rebels in the Congo and treated brutally:

> Helen Roseveare entered the pulpit holding what looked like a small shrub – large and leafy with lots of small branches. The large crowd of students listened as she described her time spent in the Congo. They heard her restrained description of the barbaric treatment she had received at the hands of the rebel soldiers. All the time she spoke, she 'absent mindedly' pulled off leaves and branches a few at a time. In the stunned silence that greeted the end of her story she put down the ragged remains and picked up an arrow. As she turned it over in her hand she said, 'What I held before was good for nothing; this can hit its intended target' and then quoted from John 15.2: 'Every branch that bears fruit he prunes, that it may bear more fruit.'[7]

From years back a friend of mine still remembers the electric atmosphere that was created when the late David Watson took a paper on which was written 'God's offer of free forgiveness' and tore it to pieces to the accompaniment of 'Too busy', 'Not interested', 'Too good to be true' – one tear per comment. The strategy was worthy of Jeremiah breaking the pot.

## 5. THE OBJECT IN MOVEMENT AND PATTERN

The last two examples demonstrate how an object may communicate not so much by its iconic quality as by playing a part in a continuing story. It is the dynamic relation between object and movement which creates a pattern and carries the meaning.

In two books which are full of ideas for using objects, Sharon Swain suggests representing the relationship between God and yourself by two chairs.[8] I have used this idea on a number of occasions and have found that people are more than willing to get involved. One chair stands for God and the other for you. In how many different ways can you position them, and what does each position mean? This is one of the many ways in which small churches have an advantage over large since members of the congregation can come out and reposition the chairs, making an explanatory comment as they do. The preacher can then weave these together into the sermon. For example, the chairs may be arranged facing each other in confrontation or rebuke, or slightly at an angle suggesting counselling and concern. Either chair can be turned away from the other ('He seems not to be listening' or 'You need to turn round and repent') or set side by side as best friends or one on top of the other ('Get off my back' or 'I carried you'). The chairs can be close together or set far apart. Other objects can come in between. The list isn't quite endless but invites creative thought before and during the sermon. The results can be amusing, uncomfortable and encouraging. The chairs do not really remind us of God or ourselves. It's the relationship between them which bears the meaning.

Similarly, in a sermon on forgiveness, the preacher invited the congregation to view his collection of grudges. These consisted of tin boxes and cans. He brought them out one by one, explaining what each stood for. The script proceeded along these lines:

> Here's my collection of grudges. I hold on to these. Each one holds
> a memory for me. Some of them I've had for a long, long time.
> Look, this is box number one. It's my sister who called me 'Dopey
> dishwater drinker'. I was only six at the time but I'll never let it go.
> This one's a teacher who made me stand in the corridor for
> laughing, when I wasn't. This one's quite recent. I only got it last
> week. It's my friend who said, 'You're always moaning. You're like a
> wet week in Manchester.' And this one's the driver who cut me up
> at the roundabout last Tuesday.

As he spoke, the preacher collected more and more boxes until his arms were full. He continued:

> I get these out every week and I look inside and I think about them
> and I polish them. I like my grudges. I hug them to myself. I'd be
> lost without them. They're the best collection in the world and
> they're all mine.
> Of course, they do get in the way. And they do weigh me down.
> And my hands are so full that I can't do anything useful. And God
> can't give me his gifts because I've got no hands free.
> The trouble is – Jesus says, 'Forgive. Let them go. Drop them.'
> So watch. I'm going to let my grudges go. Let them drop.

The tin boxes and cans were dropped one by one. Some were released only after an intense struggle but all of them made a satisfying noise as they hit the floor. At the end the sermon made two final points:

> In a minute we're going to share the Peace. The Peace says, 'Empty hands. Look. I've nothing against you. I'm not holding a grudge. We're friends. I've let it go.' The other thing we're going to do is come to Communion. At the rail, if my hands are empty, God can fill them with good things. Just look at your hands before the Peace and before Communion. Are they empty? 'Forgive us our sins because we forgive those who sin against us.'

---

**EXERCISE**

*What use can you make of a mobile phone or a bottle opener in a sermon?*

---

# PART 4

*The Word embodied in the listeners*

# 17 Whose sermon is it anyway?

## Preaching with the congregation

Sometimes preaching feels like dropping words into a black hole in space. It would be nice to get a reaction. The congregation in the synagogue at Nazareth rushed Jesus to the top of the hill in an attempt to derail his message. The Sanhedrin stopped their ears, yelled at the top of their voices and pelted Stephen with stones. Perhaps these responses were over-energetic. But some reaction would be encouraging. Anything rather than the blank stare of those catching up on their sleep, planning their holidays or wondering if they turned the gas off.

Often, of course, worshippers will say something as they walk past us at the door. But their comments do not always leave the preacher fulfilled or feeling he or she has done a good job. Here is a list of remarks made by worshippers on the way out. There are 13; I made up five of them but, terrifyingly, the other eight are genuine. I leave you to guess which are which.

- 'Good sermon vicar. You kept me on the verge of consciousness.'
- 'Did you know that there are 129 panes of glass in the east window?'
- 'It *is* quite a difficult passage. Thanks for trying.'
- 'Did you know that you remind me of Aled Jones?'
- 'I so enjoyed visiting this morning. Where can I get a piano like that one?'
- 'You're not as good as your wife.'
- 'What's the matter? Is your husband ill?'
- 'Not bad at all for a woman.'
- 'Would you say your interpretation was pre-, post- or a-millennial? Can we meet to discuss it?'
- 'Has anyone ever said what a good preacher you are? No? Well, think about it!'
- (Reproachfully) 'I'm out of hospital now, vicar' (*thinks:* 'and you

didn't come to visit me. Don't they teach mind-reading in college these days?').

- 'That was much better. Last time you were terrible.'
- 'I got a bit lost. Can you run it past me again? *Who* was it rose from the dead?'

These comments are discouraging not primarily because they dent the ego of the preacher but because they indicate that the listeners have responded *only* to the preacher. When we started to preach, our hope was that through human words, the listeners would hear and respond to the Word of God. It is a serious matter if, in the ministry of the Word, the really important *divine* Word has not been heard. And yet we all recognize that often this is precisely what seems to be happening. What can we do about it?

We may ask, 'Whose sermon is it, anyway?' We are the ones who spent time on it, sweated blood over it and will be criticized for it. It must be ours. Not so. Wherever the sermon began, it will become *the congregation's sermon*, whether we like it or not. Each will hear what they will hear and interpret and apply our words in personal and idiosyncratic ways. Once we have spoken the words we are more or less powerless to control what happens to them. But my main point is that we should be glad that the congregation will take the sermon over. We should be planning for this to happen. The sermon is worthless until it is detached from us and owned by the hearers.

In a striking phrase, James Nieman has argued for more 'preaching that drives people from the church – to spread the good news that they have heard'. He goes on, 'Unless the message becomes embedded in the lives of the hearers, it will never leave the four walls of the church. The issue is: what enables hearers to be carried away by what they hear?'[1]

## CREATING A CULTURE OF EXPECTATION

We could start here. I recall reading an unpublished piece of research which contrasted the motives for attending church services in two different congregations. In one, worshippers commented on their duty to attend or expressed a wish 'to meet with like-minded people'. In the other, most people interviewed spoke of 'coming to meet with God'. The difference in motive is enough to create two cultures, one where the sermon is an endurance test, the other where it is an opportunity to hear God speak.

The responsibility for nourishing a culture of listening is partly the preacher's. I remember discussing with a teacher of preaching the business of evaluating students' sermons. He said, 'I always try to begin, before saying anything else, by stating "I heard God speak to me in your sermon" (that's if I did and I usually do).' This intrigued me. Such an opening imprints on the student the vital point about preaching – the preacher must intend that people should hear God's Word and not be surprised if they do. The tutor was modelling an important attitude. If a preacher expects nothing and plans for nothing, it's likely nothing will happen. If a preacher colludes with the congregation in its assumption that sermons are boring and irrelevant, then the sermon begins by having to make up a great deal of lost ground.

If, on the other hand, the preacher has prepared conscientiously and prayed faithfully, he or she may begin in the faith that God wants to bless the words. This assumption will inform the introduction, bring energy and confidence to the delivery, and shape the whole perspective of the preacher. We all could do with encouragement to listen attentively. I remember one preacher who interspersed the points of the sermon with the question: 'Is that the word God brought you to hear?' Asked every week, the question would soon irritate, but in its context it kept our minds on the possibility that God had a particular word for us.

Another way of encouraging expectation is to preach from time to time on how to listen to sermons. Here is the beginning of a sermon on the parable of the Sower, a passage which has much to say about listening:

> Imagine the scene. It's not an uncommon one. A harassed mother trying to get the children to the morning service. Breakfast has been shoved down, the vegetables not done for lunch. There's been World War III over what clothes everyone is prepared to wear, ending with the explosion: 'Yes!!! You do have to go!' They make it in time – just – well, two minutes into the first hymn. The service moves into the Children's Slot and is successfully negotiated, with only one tricky moment when the second son has to have his ray-gun confiscated. The children disappear for their groups. And so to the sermon . . .
>   What does mum need most at that moment?

Here are some possible answers:

- To hear a soothing voice saying, 'Go to sleep'.
- To have a chance to re-live the argument with her teenage daughter, honing the cutting phrase which didn't come out right the first time.
- Ten minutes to work through the logistics of Monday evening, which involves getting back from work, picking up and dropping off numerous offspring and still managing a run before tea.
- To hear something to entertain her. A decent joke would help.
- To hear anything memorable. 'So often,' she thinks, 'I go into the next hymn disappointed, guilty, frustrated, angry.'

But there is something more important than all this. She needs to hear that God is desperate to communicate with her. The sower broadcasts the seed. God says, 'I want to make contact. I want to say something to you, to speak to you in the middle of your harassment and tiredness and your sense of having heard it all before.'

Just as she herself phones the eldest daughter at college and says, 'I saw this and thought of you.'

Just as she meets a friend in town and says, 'Let's go for coffee.'

God wants to speak to her – she needs to know that more than anything else.

We need to know that.

And this morning, you need to know that.

## AIMING FOR CELEBRATION

Is it possible to go further and help the congregation to begin the process of owning the sermon during the sermon itself? The sermon is a celebration of the grace and love of God. Can we celebrate along with those listening?

### The communication loop

Much depends on how we begin. Watching the experts at communicating – Eddie Izzard, Billy Connolly, Peter Ustinov – I was struck by how skilfully they established a rapport with the audience. I assume that very often the irrelevant joke with which many sermons begin has this as its purpose. No doubt gratuitous humour has its place, but the sense that this preacher is serious, has something important and relevant to say and is personally involved in the message will probably do the same job as effectively. Robert Pagliari writes of the 'communication loop' that is set up between preacher and congregation.

> The initial 'charge' that sets this loop in motion has to come from the preacher. If the preacher initiates this communication cycle with a bolt of enthusiasm, the congregation responds and returns a larger bolt of enthusiasm to the preacher. This further 'energizes' the preacher who sends more enthusiasm back to the congregation and so on. The loop becomes more and more 'electrical', and the turn-around time quicker and quicker, to the point where the cycle is so great and so rapid that communication becomes communion.[2]

## Participant proclamation

It is worth noting that Pagliari is speaking out of the Roman Catholic tradition. Celebration during the sermon is a phenomenon which we have come to associate more with black congregations. So Evans Crawford writes of 'participant proclamation', the assumption that the listeners will respond vocally to the word preached.

> The sermon belongs not only to the preacher but to the entire congregation, which joins in with their oral responses . . . The congregation's participation may sometimes arise from a desire to change the phenomenon. 'Help 'em, Lord!' is not a prayer of objective observation! The observers become active participants who encourage the Spirit and the preacher to bring forth the word of God more clearly.[3]

He suggests that participant proclamation is one of the ways in which we can observe the priesthood of all believers in action. As the congregation demonstrates its investment in the sermon, so 'the misery of feeling alone in the pulpit ceases'. Preacher and congregation perform the sermon together.

# INTERACTING WITH THE CONGREGATION

So are there ways in which the insights of black preaching about participation can be incorporated into other worship traditions? In some traditions preachers encourage congregations to respond by finishing their sentences. I was once present in a New York church full of high-salaried professionals. Yet the preacher preached a series of short sentences, each of which ended with the words 'He touched me, he touched me.' I was fascinated to see that people unselfconsciously finished the phrase for him.

Much more common in my experience, is the question which is really an invitation to the congregation to affirm what is said. 'If anyone is in Christ, there is a new creation! Right?' Back came the response: 'Right!' Is this difficult for traditionally minded congregations? Perhaps no more than: 'The Lord is here!' 'His Spirit is with us!'

We should not be afraid of asking real questions during the sermon. Most preachers have had the unnerving experience of asking a rhetorical question and getting it answered! But both Jesus and Paul appear to have expected their listeners to engage with them. Walter Hollenweger even refers to Jesus as the 'dialogic Christ'. Why should we not encourage and expect response from those who are listening to us?

Recently I have heard a preacher ask: 'How many of you have been really disappointed by not getting something you really hoped for?' The preacher didn't expect anyone to state publicly the nature of the disappointment. But by putting up their hands, some at least of those listening engaged with the sermon. I've heard other preachers ask people to indicate whether they thought repentance was a matter of the mind or the heart or whether they were on the side of Paul or Barnabas in the dispute over John Mark in Acts 15.36–41.

A much more didactic method is that of the sermon outline. Here the listeners are encouraged to fill in the blank spaces in the outline. Sometimes it will mean no more than a biblical reference; sometimes a pause will allow people to jot down a thought or a personal example; sometimes the preacher may invite the congregation to record a key phrase. Some congregations may find this patronizing. I'm inclined to say that it all depends on what you ask people to do and how you ask them.

Another preacher broke off in the middle of a sermon on Jesus' healing ministry to run though a dozen sayings of Jesus (for example: 'Neither do

I condemn you; go and sin no more' or 'Peace be still' or 'Launch out into the deep') and invited the hearers to consider if any one of these sayings was a personal word to them.

We shouldn't be too quick to dismiss these ways of encouraging response within the sermon. Laurence Wagley observes: 'Jesus' preaching was participatory. It grew out of the lives of the people, used shared conversations as a common vehicle and discovered the grace of God in social encounters.'[4] I think it is a style of preaching made for the small congregation. Wagley comments: 'We have never developed a preaching method designed just for the small membership church', but preaching that is participatory and invites response *works best* in the small church.

## SHARING THE SERMON

Three recent studies have suggested other ways in which the congregation can interact with the preacher during the sermon.

Jeremy Thomson's *Preaching as Dialogue* lists practical strategies for making the sermon explicitly dialogical. His suggestions cover three different types of response. First, the preacher can *invite questions* at the end of a usual sermon or, greatly daring, stop for questions in the course of the sermon. Alternatively, he or she might hold up the argument of the sermon to allow for *a contribution, personal insight or relevant experience* by which the congregation can illustrate a sermonic point. Or, the preacher might break the sermon to invite listeners either in pairs or groups to react to what they have heard so far and feed the results back into the sermon.[5]

Tim Stratford's *Interactive Preaching* invites a riskier strategy. He suggests that the preacher opens the sermon but then pauses to leave space for the congregation to contribute its own reactions, questions and stories. He argues that, though this approach may leave the preacher feeling vulnerable, the big advantage is that contributions will reflect the real life of the congregation and not the preacher's private cupboard of illustrations. At the end of the time of sharing, the preacher still has the responsibility of tying up loose ends and landing the sermon safely.[6]

This policy clearly demands much of the preacher and is probably easier to operate with 25 worshippers than 200-plus. It will not be possible entirely to predict the direction the contributions will take, and making a nourishing meal out of the assorted scraps that are thrown into the pot will take quick thinking, imagination and reliance on the Spirit of God.

A third approach is that suggested by Brian Pearson. He writes about his experiments with dramatic presentations during the sermon. He sets up the scene, allows the action to unfold but then begins to ask the 'actors' 'what they think is going on, why their character is behaving in a certain way, what their character might be feeling, and where this might lead'. This seems to me a very risky strategy but he writes enthusiastically about its possibilities. He observes that the method provokes many post-sermon conversations, and not all of them with him as preacher. In other words, 'People want to talk to the "characters". The observers too have been drawn into the scene. The sermon lives on!'[7]

However nerve-wracking this might be, Thomson's, Stratford's and Pearson's suggestions help us turn towards the congregation. This chapter began with the question, 'Whose sermon is it anyway?' The sermon does not have to be six feet above contradiction. It is easy to give out the unspoken message that the preacher is removed from the real-life experiences of the congregation and to imply that it is incapable of thinking about faith in an adult way. A different message is communicated when the preacher invites the congregation to get involved. As a culture of listening attentively and expecting to contribute develops, so we can hope that more and more congregations will take it for granted that the sermon is not a time to sleep and will begin to make it their own. Such preaching drives people from the church in a positive way as the preacher's words become embodied in the hearers.

---

**EXERCISE**

*It is possible that some of my suggestions seem hopelessly unrealistic in your context. What steps could you take to encourage the congregations that you work with to interact with your preaching?*

---

# 18 Contributing to the Feast

*Preaching for a response*

The previous chapter outlined some of the ways in which the preacher can encourage a culture of participation and shared celebration with the congregation. In this chapter I want to explore different kinds of response once the sermon is over – both within the service and afterwards.

The assumption that the sermon requires a response reflects the centrifugal nature of the Good News. At the end of Matthew's Gospel Jesus sends the disciples into all the world to do something. It's not a suggestion about sunbathing. During his ministry Jesus often commanded people to declare themselves in some way. For example, the question 'Who touched me?' was intended to flush out a nervous woman so that she could tell everyone that she had been healed (Luke 8.42–48). The Bible is not designed to tickle our fancy or provide us with material for endless late-night discussions. Jesus' saying, 'He that hath ears to hear, let him hear' can be rendered 'If you've got ears, use them!'

What kind of responses are possible? In an excellent booklet on responding to preaching, John Leach lists some types of response – conversion, sanctification, reconciliation, healing, 'anointing' or equipping, practical action, moral and ethical responses, longing for God.'[1]

But however we draw the map, the kind of response which we think appropriate will affect the purpose, direction and conclusion of the sermon.

## RESPONSES AFTER THE SERMON AND DURING THE SERVICE

### Prayer

The commonest response to the sermon is probably still the preacher's prayer. Rather than a perfunctory line or two or a hasty doxology, it would be worth making time for a period of silence when the congregation can reflect on what it has heard and turn one thought into a personal and private prayer.

An alternative is for the preacher to offer biddings which pick out key ideas in the sermon (without making them sound like a revision test for those who haven't been following). Such prayer opportunities can cover a variety of responses – confession, devotion, commitment, longing for a deeper experience of God. Many churches set aside time at this point for an extended period of prayer and anointing. This is a common custom on Maundy Thursday, but there is no reason why it should be restricted to this occasion.

## Affirmations of faith

Some traditions build saying the creed into their services every week. Like all rituals, it can become a thoughtless habit. Nevertheless there are some times when declaring (rather than reciting) an affirmation of faith may be exactly the response that the sermon calls for. This is because part of what we do in worship can be termed 'defiant proclamation'. Walter Brueggemann puts it well in a comment on Psalm 96's confident cry: 'The Lord is King.'

> When the Church says the name of Yahweh, out loud, under its breath it also says quietly but undoubtedly, 'and not Baal, not Marduk, not Dagon, not Enlil, not, not, not'. Doxology to Yahweh attacks the claim of every other god and every other loyalty. Israel freely confesses that the other gods have no gifts to give, no benefits to bestow, no summons to make, no allegiance to claim. They are massively and forcefully dismissed.[2]

Of course, the moment needs to be properly framed. The congregation declares its allegiance to God as a deliberate act of defiant protest. This is not a time for a tired shuffling to one's feet and lack-lustre droning. In some churches it may be possible to compose one's own affirmation of faith or act of commitment, tailored to the specific sermon and the occasion.

## Praise

Very often the most appropriate response to the sermon will be an extended time of joyful praise allowing the congregation to embody its reception of the good news. Here we can learn from the tradition of black

169

preaching which strongly emphasizes the role of celebration as the proper climax of preaching. Henry Mitchell, himself a legendary black preacher writes:

> We in African American tradition have cultural roots which demand that a sermon end in a celebration. For this we had a number of our own terms, such as 'coming on up at the end', 'the gravy', 'the rousements', 'the whoop' or just the generic 'climax'. We knew celebration to be so essential that no sermon dared end without one.[3]

'No sermon dared end without one.' All this may seem a million miles away from the average church service, but it points us in the right direction. Of course we need to be careful about pushing people out of their comfort zone and making the service an occasion for embarrassment but there is something liberating about Mitchell's defence of celebration: 'Joy is the most contagious thing I know of . . . The movement of hearers is by contagion. People are led, not pushed, into genuine celebration.'[4]

## The Peace

I realize that not every tradition includes the Peace in worship. In those which do, it is important to explain its purpose. I have been surprised by the number of people who seem to have little idea of its significance. When properly introduced and understood, the Peace can be the perfect response to a sermon on unity, forgiveness or reconciliation. It is a pity that, in the Anglican tradition, recent versions of the invitation to Communion omit the words: 'ye that do truly and earnestly repent of your sins and are *in love and charity with your neighbours*, draw near with faith . . .' The Peace, far from being get-to-know-you-better time, should be a profound expression of the unity of the body of Christ and a challenge to be reconciled with any fellow Christians from whom one is estranged.

## Holy Communion

Holy Communion is the way par excellence of responding to the Word preached. The sermon can naturally lead into the moment when worshippers take bread and wine in memory of Jesus' death and feed on his life. The Communion takes us back into the 'night in which Jesus was betrayed', it speaks of a body broken and blood poured out, it looks forward to Christ's coming again and the messianic banquet, it emphasizes the unity of all who gather around the table. The service does all this even if the sermon doesn't mention any of these elements. But the sermon can highlight one or another of them and can bring a fresh experience of God's love and a renewed understanding of his grace out of a ritual which most worshippers will have experienced hundreds of times. The sermon has the potential to make this particular celebration personal and specific. It may not always make a direct connection with Communion but it's worth asking on every occasion if there is some way in which word can illuminate sacrament.

## Symbolic actions

There are many kinds of symbolic action and the list which follows is a tiny sample of what is possible.[5]

1  One preacher ended the sermon with a time of prayer but invited people to stand if God had spoken to them in the sermon. Since the worshippers had their eyes shut for the prayer this invitation was less threatening than it might otherwise have been. But standing or raising a hand (a safer alternative) fixed the response in the minds of those whom God had touched.

2  A Christmas sermon on the shepherds ended with the preacher distributing pieces of paper to half a dozen volunteers. On each piece was written: 'Unto you is born this day a saviour who is Christ the Lord. Pass it on.' The preacher continued:

> Can I have a few volunteers to help me with one last little activity? One of the things that strikes me about the shepherds was just how eager they were to respond to what God said and to pass it on. If something means a great deal to us we want to share it with others, especially good news. Pass the papers around. It works best if everyone does it. The shepherds did it in their way – you can do it in your way.[6]

3  Many churches make use of a prayer tree. The large outline of a tree is displayed at the front. The congregation writes out short prayers on stick-on notes or leaf-shaped pieces of paper with sticky backs. They

are then invited to come and fix their prayers on to the branches of the tree.

4   Though it takes careful organizing, it is also possible for the congregation to write prayers on stick-on notes which can be made into links to make a chain of prayer requests.

5   At one Ash Wednesday service people were invited to write down their sins (presumably only a sample!) and then in a ritual act burn the pieces of paper in a brazier set up by the door of the church. Understandably, those who took part were scrupulous about seeing that every scrap of paper was consumed in the flames.

6   A similar idea, though one fraught with fewer problems of accidental disclosure, involves taking a stone which represents a burden and putting it at the foot of the cross.

7   At an all-age service both adults and children came out to write their names on a large painting of the hands of God, thus picking up the thought in Isaiah 49.15–16: 'I will not forget you. See, I have inscribed you on the palms of my hands.'

8   Many symbolic responses involve the lighting of candles, whether as a prayer or a resolution or a way of remembering someone.

9   It is also possible to use water as a symbol, inviting people to wash their hands in a bowl or allow themselves to be sprinkled as a symbol of the Spirit and cleansing. (It's more fun to use children to do the sprinkling.) It's also fairly common for Maundy Thursday services to involve mutual foot-washing.

Not all of these examples will be to everyone's taste. They should certainly not be seen as merely artistic or theatrical; nor as a 'twee' way of ending the service. Nor are they appropriate only with children. Revivalist preaching has always known the value of asking those who wish to respond to Christ's call to 'get up out of their seats and come to the front'. What is important is the enormous power of action and symbol to imprint response to the preached Word. Word-centred traditions are sometimes reluctant to allow responses other than the spiritual, by which they often mean the cerebral and the verbal. But God has ensured that the spiritual finds a home in the body. For hundreds of years Christians have been making use of bread, wine, water, oil, flame to flesh out their deepest feelings. They have employed movement and gesture – dancing, standing, raising their hands, kneeling – to express heart-felt yearnings. Such responses have not always been linked with the sermon, however. But what is the congregation intended to do with the sermon in order to make it its own? It is entirely appropriate that the Word should find utterance in the worship of the congregation.[7]

## RESPONSES AFTER THE SERVICE

This is the point where the sermon stands or falls. What will happen to the words painstakingly prepared and faithfully spoken once the service is over and the congregation has gone home? Preaching should drive people from the church to live out the Word in their lives. How can sermons fulfil that role? Here I want to outline three different kinds of response for when the service is over.

### Seeing things differently

In the final analysis this may well be the most significant effect of a sermon. A lot of our preaching is not aimed at immediate action but at strengthening a Christian perspective on the world. This has been called 'world-view maintenance' and it consists of reminding the worshippers great truths which they already know and on which they take their stand. Hence the importance of embodied responses during the service. Actions help press the message home.

I remember a preacher who asked us to plant a bulb when we got home (he'd brought enough for one per member of the congregation). Then he encouraged us to put a stone over the spot where we had planted it. 'In the spring,' he said, 'you'll see the bulb push the stone aside and it will be a sign of the power of Christ's resurrection.' Everyone present knew of the resurrection, but his words attached a meaning to an object. Those particular places in our gardens were now bound up with thoughts of the risen Christ.

Sometimes the sermon manages to put into words what the hearers have always felt deep down but have been unable to articulate. Earlier I described Elizabeth's precious gift to Mary as naming what God was doing in her life. As a result of Elizabeth's words Mary saw the whole situation differently and burst forth in praise: 'Tell out, my soul, the greatness of the Lord!' (Luke 1.47–55). Sometimes the sermon will offer a new image for visualizing God's way with us or will disturb our cosy way of seeing the world. However it does it, skilful preaching aims to change the way we see life and inspires us to finish the sermon for ourselves and complete the story in our living.

## Taking definite action

Sometimes the sermon has an obviously practical implication and proposes specific and concrete action. It may say, 'Sign up for the coffee-making rota', 'Distribute leaflets', 'Collect Christian Aid envelopes', 'Offer to be on the catering team for Alpha', 'Come on Thursday to help clean the church', 'Give generously to this good cause', 'Sign up for this protest march'.

An unusual, some might feel shocking, approach to preaching for definite action appeared in a recent news report:

> The Bishop of Salisbury, the Rt Revd David Stancliffe, is advising clergy to withhold the blessing from congregations who do not put their Christian faith into practice. Speaking on the publication of his new book on worship, the Bishop, author of *God's Pattern: Shaping Our Worship, Ministry and Life*, added to earlier comments that church worship is often uninspiring by suggesting that the blessing could be held over churchgoers as a bribe.
>
> For example, in Christian Aid week it is perfectly proper to say, 'There are three streets that need visiting and you are not going to get a blessing until someone sticks up a hand', he told *The Times*.[8]

Not everyone will want or be able to employ the Bishop's personal brand of leverage. The strength of his suggestion is that it takes the sermon seriously as the Word of God to the congregation and assumes that God still calls his people to acts of obedience which will involve time and commitment. St Francis heard Christ calling him to rebuild the Church and took this command in the most literal sense, hauling blocks of stone to what became a building site. Sometimes Christians are cursed with the tendency to make a metaphor out of everything.

## Talking it through

I don't want to disparage talking as a proper response. After all, we often don't know what we think until we've said it. So the sermon might be followed with questions to discuss at a mid-week group or after the service (though probably not at a 'Grill the preacher' session, which can be the antithesis of responding to the call of God). The most productive groups are those where group members work hard at sharing memories, telling personal stories and teasing out practical applications.[9]

Laurence Wagley sees talking as a practical response if the discussion is purposeful. He bewails the lack of serious intent which he believes afflicts modern preaching.

> The sermon seems designed to fill 20 minutes. The congregation files out languidly with no action in mind. The church will initiate no new programs as a result of this sermon. Another sermon has been put to rest; it will have no continued life in the church.[10]

His disappointment with much contemporary preaching leads him toward what he calls participatory preaching and decision-making. Wagley clearly assumes that sermons will be followed by someone asking, 'Now the question is, what can we do? Are there any implications for how we will live our lives this week?'[11] He argues that bringing the congregation into the sermon through participating in the outcome gives the sermon purpose. In Wagley's view it is possible to open up social issues, doctrinal understanding and life situations by this method. It is even possible to explore faith evangelistically by raising existential questions, facing doubts and inviting decision – a strategy which he believes may be less manipulative than the traditional altar call.

Wagley's approach creates a culture where discussing the sermon is assumed to be the natural thing to do. This is of particular value to those who are giving church a try and may be on their way into faith. But it is also helpful for those who are drifting away from the Church. The questions which the sermon provokes are often the same for both groups. Taking post-sermon discussion for granted affirms the inquirer's search and also respects the questions of those wrestling with doubt. It is a common experience for those enduring a crisis of faith to feel that having difficulties is seriously bad for your health and rightly disapproved of by the godly. They wonder if they will be treated as if they had caught something infectious. In fact, of course, as Catherine Byrom has shown, difficulties over faith may be points of growth,[12] but in any case, little is gained by adding guilt to doubt.

So far this section has dealt with semi-formal responses. There is a lot to be said for the informal. Centuries ago John Chrysostom exhorted his congregations in these words:

> One thing, however, it is necessary for us to bid and entreat, that
> you continue to have the same zeal and manifest it not here only,
> but also when you are at home. Converse husband with wife, parent
> with child concerning these matters. Speak first of your own
> thoughts, and then ask for those of others, and in this way, all of you
> shall contribute to this excellent feast.[13]

This may call for a change of post-worship routine, but the idea is a good one. A number of people I know go off to a nearby coffee shop to talk over the sermon after morning worship. John Chrysostom would have been proud of them. It beats moaning about the hymns anyway.

The implication of this chapter is that it is not enough to prepare a sermon as if it were a way of filling up the time. Bringing congregational response into the equation forces the preacher to address demanding questions: 'What do I want to happen once I have finished speaking?', 'Can I state my aim in broad terms?', 'Can I say what I will ask the congregation to do?' Many of us are not used to thinking of sermon construction in this way. We look for a pithy summary of our main points or search for a telling story. Now it must be granted, of course, that not every sermon will call for activities as if the preacher were a teacher required to set weekly homework. But at the risk of sounding harsh, the preacher who never expects a response, never plans for one, and would be taken aback if there were one, is wasting the congregation's time.

As this book comes to an end, I realize that this is not quite what I would like the last word to be. I am struck by how much of what I have written represents building blocks. We design the sermon, hoping the structure is sound; we take time to lay foundations, to build walls, to check that the doors are hanging properly and that the windows let in the light. But that is not the end of the story. I have walked through stately homes which are beautifully appointed – and empty. A silver snuff box on a lacquered table, a chair roped off so that no one can sit down, a long dining table that will seat 20, but its highly polished surface hasn't hosted a meal in years. And I have seen other houses which have stood empty for many months, with windows broken and doors kicked in.

The building of a space for God to call his home is an important and a necessary task but it is not enough. At the dedication of the temple in 2 Chronicles 5, all those who had laboured in its construction gathered together, they made sacrifice, the priests sanctified themselves, the orchestra played with cymbals, harps, lyres and trumpets and the Levitical choirs sang their heads off. It must have been an awe-inspiring sight and a glorious sound. Such celebration in front of an empty box.

And then the Lord came.

And 'the priests could not stand to minister because of the cloud; for the glory of the Lord filled the house of God' (2 Chronicles 5.13–14). In the end that's the only embodiment that matters.

# Notes

## Chapter 1

1 John Bunyan, *Seasonable Counsel*, pp. 25–6, quoted in Gordon Mursell, *English Spirituality: From Earliest Times to 1700* (London: SPCK, 2001), pp. 408–9. The punctuation of the passage is mine.

2 Walter Burghardt, *Preaching: the Art and the Craft* (New York/Mahwah: Paulist Press, 1987), p. 15.

3 Stephen E. Fowl and L. Gregory Jones, *Reading in Communion: Scripture and Ethics in Christian Life* (Grand Rapids: Eerdmans Publishing Co., 1991), p. 34.

4 Calvin Miller, *Spirit, Word and Story: A Philosophy of Marketplace Preaching* (Grand Rapids: Baker Books, 1989; 2nd edition 1996), p. 153.

5 For a collection of key articles in the field of homiletics see David Day, Jeff Astley and Leslie Francis (eds), *A Reader on Preaching: Making Connections* (Aldershot: Ashgate, 2005).

6 Calvin Miller, *Spirit, Word and Story*, p. 172.

## Chapter 2

1 George Herbert, 'The windows' in Donald Davie (ed.), *The New Oxford Book of Christian Verse* (Oxford: Oxford University Press, 1981), pp. 76–7.

2 Quoted by Hans Urs von Balthasar in *Communio* (Vol. 24, 1997), p. 371.

3 C. H. Spurgeon, *Lectures to My Students* (London: Passmore and Alabaster, 1875), pp. 12–13.

4 C. H. Spurgeon, *Lectures to My Students*, p. 13.

5 James R. Nieman, 'Preaching that drives people from the church', in *Currents in Theology and Mission* (Vol. 20, 1993), pp. 106–15.

6 H. Begbie, *William Booth: Founder of the Salvation Army* (2 volumes) (London: Macmillan, 1920), Vol. 1, p. 228.

7 Robert Pagliari, *Fourteen Steps to Dynamic Preaching* (Liguori: Liguori Publications, 1993), p. 47.

8 Richard F. Ward, *Speaking from the Heart: Preaching with Passion* (Nashville: Abingdon, 1992), pp. 24–5.

9 Martyn Lloyd-Jones, *Preaching and Preachers* (London: Hodder and Stoughton, 1971), p. 88.

10 Martyn Lloyd-Jones, *Preaching and Preachers*, p. 97.

11 I cannot trace the reference to this anecdote but I am grateful to Revd Dale Hanson for the substance of the story.

12 Quoted in Paul Wesley Chilcote, *She Offered Them Christ*, first published by Abingdon (1993), p. 53, reprinted by Wipf and Stock Publishers, Orlando (2001), but originally from John Wesley, *The Journal of the Rev John Wesley, A. M.*, ed. Nehemiah Curnock, 8 vols. (London: Epworth Press, 1909–16), Vol. 3, p. 250.

13 Thomas G. Long, 'The distance we have travelled: changing trends in preaching', in *Reformed Liturgy and Music* (No. 17, 1983), pp. 11–15.

14 Ben Campbell Johnson and Andrew Dreitcer, *Beyond the Ordinary: Spirituality for Church Leaders* (Grand Rapids, Michigan; and Cambridge, England: William B. Eerdmans Publishing Co., 1989), pp. 134–6.

15 Karl Barth, *Homiletics*, trans. G. W. Bromily and D. E. Daniels (Louisville: Westminster/John Knox Press, 1991), p. 84.

16 Calvin Miller, *Spirit, Word and Story: A Philosophy of Marketplace Preaching* (Grand Rapids: Baker Books, 1989), pp. 216–18.

17 Walter Burghart, *Preaching: The Art and the Craft* (New York/Mahwah: Paulist Press, 1987), p. 16.

**Chapter 3**

1 From an unpublished sermon by Catherine Byrom.

2 Rebecca Dolch, 'Offer them Christ: the Blood of Christ', sermon excerpt, November 1987, quoted in Carol Noren, *The Woman in the Pulpit* (Nashville: Abingdon, 1991), p. 72.

3 Beverly J. Shamana, 'Letting go', in Ella Pearson Mitchell (ed.), *Those Preachin' Women* (Valley Forge: Judson, 1985), p. 75.

4 James A. Feehan, *Preaching in Stories* (Dublin: Mercier Press, 1989), pp. 23ff.

5 David Buttrick, *Homiletic: Moves and Structures* (Philadelphia: Fortress Press, 1997), pp. 142ff.

6 In the sermon, 'Our God is able', in *Strength to Love* (New York: Evanston; London: Harper and Row, 1963), pp. 101–7.

7 Calvin Miller, *Spirit, Word and Story: A Philosophy of Marketplace Preaching* (Grand Rapids: Baker Books, 2nd edition, 1996), p. 182.

8 Ernst Kasemann, 'The saving significance of Jesus' death in the letters of Paul', in *Perspectives on Paul* (Philadelphia: Fortress Press, 1971), p. 38.

9 John 9.25.

10 See, for example, Philippians 3.4–11 and 2 Corinthians 12.2–10.

11 Tim Keel, 'Christianity as intimacy', in *Christianity Today International/Leadership Journal* (Winter 2005, Vol. 26, No. 1), p. 78.

12 Cheryl J. Sanders, 'The woman as preacher', *Journal of Religious Thought* (Vol. 43, No. 1, 1986), pp. 6–23.

13 Heather Walton and Susan Durber (eds), *Silence in Heaven: A Book of Women's Preaching* (London: SCM, 1994), p. xvi.

14 Carol Noren, *The Woman in the Pulpit* (Nashville: Abingdon, 1991), p. 30.

15 I have been unable to trace this quotation. It was drawn to my attention by Revd Michael Wilcock, who read it some years ago in the magazine *Decision*. Presumably it comes from Spurgeon's *Lectures to My Students* but I should be grateful for the reference.

## Chapter 4

1 Paul Scott Wilson, *The Practice of Preaching* (Nashville: Abingdon, 1995), pp. 133–4.

2 Stephen Farris, *Preaching That Matters* (Louisville: Westminster John Knox, 1998), pp. 72–4.

3 David Day, 'Beyond the sacred page', in *A Preaching Workbook* (London: SPCK/Lynx, 1998), pp. 22–32.

4 Barbara Brown Taylor, *The Preaching Life* (Boston: Cowley Publishing, 1993), p. 48.

5 John Goldingay, *An Ignatian Approach to Reading the Old Testament* (Grove Biblical Series B24, Cambridge: Grove Books, 2002), p. 7.

6 All the quotations from Ignatius are taken from Halcyon Backhouse (ed.), *The Spiritual Exercises of St Ignatius of Loyola* (London: Hodder and Stoughton, 1989).

7 Charles Rice, 'Shaping sermons by the interplay of text and metaphor', in Don M. Wardlow (ed.), *Preaching Biblically* (Philadelphia: Westminster, 1983), p. 104.

8 From David Day, *Pearl Beyond Price* (Harrow: Zondervan, 2001), p. 181.

9 Barbara Brown Taylor, 'The reign of God is like . . .', in Roger Alling and David Schlafer (eds), *Preaching Through the Year of Matthew: Sermons That Work X* (Harrisburg: Morehouse, 2001), p. ix.

10 Barbara Brown Taylor, *The Preaching Life*, p. 47.

11 Ezekiel 3.3; Jeremiah 15.16.

12 My thanks to Kate Ross for this sermon.

13 Thomas Troeger, *Imagining a Sermon* (Nashville: Abingdon, 1990), chapter 3.

14 Walter Wink, *Transforming Bible Study* (Nashville: Abingdon, 1980; London: SCM, 1991), p. 64.

15 From a workshop exercise devised by Geoffrey Stevenson.

16 For Dennis Dewey's website see www.dennisdewey.org.

## Chapter 5

1 Martyn Lloyd-Jones, *Preaching and Preachers* (London: Hodder and Stoughton, 1971), p. 58.

2 From a sermon by Susan Durber at a College of Preachers' Conference, Swanwick, April 2004.

3 From a sermon preached in St John's College, Durham.

4 Jeremy Davies, 'The Annunciation', *The Times Book of Best Sermons* (London: Cassell, 1995), p. 7.

## Chapter 6

1 Alison Peacock, 'Crossing the border', in HeatherWalton and Susan Durber (eds), *Silence in Heaven* (London: SCM, 1994), p. 119.

2 Barbara BrownTaylor, *Home by AnotherWay* (Boston: Cowley Publications, 1999), p. 75.

3 Henry Mitchell, *Celebration and Experience in Preaching* (Nashville: Abingdon Press, 1990), pp. 91–3.

4 Katharine Jefferts Schori, *The Nag*, in Roger Alling and David Schlafer (eds), *Preaching Through theYear of Luke: Sermons ThatWork IX* (Harrisburg: Morehouse Publishing, 2000), pp. 150–3.

5 John L. Pritchard, 'All or nothing', in *Living the Gospel Stories Today* (London: SPCK Triangle, 2001), p. 65.

6 Henry Mitchell, *Black Preaching* (San Francisco: Harper and Row, 1979), p. 206 (from a sermon by Dr Sandy F. Ray).

7 Kathy Galloway, *Getting Personal: Sermons and Meditations (1986–94)* (London: SPCK, 1995), pp. 107–8.

## Chapter 7

1 Bill Bryson, *A Short History of Nearly Everything* (London: Transworld Publishers; Black Swan edition, 2004), pp. 351–2.

2 Eva Feder Kittay, *Metaphor: Its Cognitive Force and Linguistic Structure* (Chicago: University of Chicago, 1987), p. 316.

3 For an illuminating account of radio preachers like C. S. Lewis, AngelaTilby and Rabbi Lionel Blue and their use of pictorial language, see Jolyon Mitchell, *Visually Speaking* (Edinburgh: T. andT. Clark, 1999), pp. 88–127.

4 Barbara Brown Taylor, 'Preaching the body', in Gail R. O'Day and Thomas G. Long (eds), *Listening to theWord* (Nashville: Abingdon, 1993), p. 215.

5 From a sermon by Revd Penny Martin.

6 Bishop John Pritchard, Maundy Thursday sermon, Durham Cathedral, 2002.

7 StephenWright, 'Cliché corner', in *Journal of the College of Preachers* (January 2000), p. 15.

8 SeeWayne McDill, *The Twelve Essential Skills for Great Preachers* (Nashville: Broadman and Holman Publishers, 1994), pp. 201–17.

## Chapter 8

1 Jolyon Mitchell, 'Finding life amid death', in Ruth Gledhill (ed.), *The Fourth Times Book of Best Sermons* (London: Cassell, 1999), pp. 26–31.

2 Raynor Anderson, 'A life not our own' (John 14.8–17), in Roger Alling and David Schlafer (eds), *Preaching Through the Year of Matthew: Sermons That Work X* (Harrisburg, Pennsylvania: Morehouse Publishing, 2001), pp. 62–4.

3 Martha Anderson, 'There is need of only one thing', in Roger Alling and David Schlafer (eds), *Preaching Through theYear of Luke: Sermons ThatWork X*, (Harrisburg, Pennsylvania: Morehouse Publishing, 2000), pp. 62–4.

4    Victoria Wood, 'Nora', in *Barmy* (London: Methuen, 1987), p. 15.
5    John S. McClure, *The Four Codes of Preaching* (Minneapolis: Fortress Press, 1991), p. 137.

### Chapter 9

1    We are not surprised to find in *The Life of St Confitura* that a mystical saint, easily provoked, covered in lard with a penchant for garlic, is described as 'a super slimy, fragile mystic, plagued with halitosis'.
2    Thomas Hefferson, *Sacred Biography* (New York/Oxford: Oxford University Press, 1988), p. 157.
3    Jane Speck, 'Into the lake of lions: medieval women and bodily suffering', in *Borderlands* (Issue 1, Summer 2002), pp. 36–7, 43.
4    Mark Barger Elliott, 'When God is absent', in *Creative Styles of Preaching* (Westminster John Knox Press, 2000), pp. 83–6.
5    Fleming Rutledge, 'The thankful life', in *The Bible and the New York Times* (Grand Rapids: Eerdmans, 1998), pp. 20–4.
6    Mark Greene's work on discipleship in the workplace and on the importance of encouraging people in their ministry at work is well known and deserves to be better known. See, among many books, Mark Greene, *Thank God It's Monday* (Bletchley: Scripture Union, 3rd edition, 2003).

### Chapter 10

1    Jim Bell (Conference Leader), *A Stronghold for Men*, unpublished conference booklet, Gartmore House, 24–26 May 2002, p. 20.
2    Many years ago a technique involving dilemmas was employed in a project on Moral Education in Schools, based, as I remember, at Lancaster University. As defined by the project, a dilemma was a carefully constructed case study consisting of a central character in a readily understood context faced with a conflict of values.
3    James Lawrence, *Lost for Words* (Oxford: Bible Reading Fellowship, 1999), p. 65.
4    Barbara Brown Taylor, 'Preaching the body', in Gail R. O'Day and Thomas G. Long (eds), *Listening to the Word* (Nashville: Abingdon, 1993), p. 221
5    Mark Greene, *Thank God It's Monday* (Bletchley: Scripture Union, 3rd edition, 2003), p. 77.

### Chapter 11

1    See, for example, Roger Standing, *Finding the Plot: Preaching in Narrative Style* (Milton Keynes: Paternoster Press, 2004); Joel Green and Michael Pasquarello III (eds), *Narrative Reading, Narrative Preaching* (Grand Rapids: Baker Academic, 2003); Richard S. Eslinger, *Narrative Imagination: Preaching the Worlds That Shape Us* (Minneapolis: Fortress Press, 1995); and three books by Eugene L. Lowry: *The Homiletical Plot: The Sermon as Narrative Art Form* (Atlanta: John Knox, 1980); *How to Preach a Parable: Designs for*

*Narrative Sermons* (Nashville: Abingdon Press, 1989); *The Sermon: Dancing the Edge of Mystery* (Nashville: Abingdon, 1997).

2 Joe McKeever, Sermon Workshop.

3 Soren Kierkegaard, *Journals 1834–1854* (ed. and trans. by Alexander Dru) (London and Glasgow: Collins, Fontana, 1958), pp. 252–3.

4 For a whole volume devoted to these ways of using stories, see Eugene Lowry's *How to Preach a Parable: Designs for Narrative Sermons.*

5 William Willimon, 'One tough master?', in W. Willimon and S. Hauerwas, *Preaching to Strangers* (Westminster: John Knox, 1992), pp. 79–89.

## Chapter 12

1 From a sermon by Kate Macpherson.

2 John Vannorsdall, 'The elder son's defense', in Thomas G. Long and Cornelius Plantinga, Jr (eds), *A Chorus of Witnesses* (Grand Rapids: Eerdmans, 1994), pp. 204–11.

3 Jerry Camery-Hoggatt, *Speaking of God* (Peabody: Hendrickson, 1995), pp. 195–204.

## Chapter 13

1 Source: Broadcasters' Audience Research Board Ltd. These figures were accurate at the time of writing, though *EastEnders* soon afterwards began to experience a crisis in viewing figures.

2 Alison Graham, *Radio Times,* 27 May–2 June 2000.

3 Philip Hensher, 'Everyone should have a soap opera in their life', in *The Friday Review, The Independent,* 18 February 2000, p. 5.

4 Victor Turner, *Dramas, Fields and Metaphors: Symbolic Action in Human Society* (Ithaca: Cornell University Press, 1974).

5 Clive Marsh and Gaye W. Oritz (eds), *Explorations in Theology and Film: Movies and Meaning* (Oxford: Blackwell, 1997).

6 Gerd Theissen has tried to construct a framework consisting of basic motifs of biblical faith which will allow us to lay biblical concepts alongside ideas emerging from the raw material of the soap world. See Gerd Theissen, *The Sign Language of Faith* (London: SCM, 1995), pp. 17–22.

7 For a stimulating analysis of secular, quasi-religious beliefs, see the series by Don Cupitt: *The New Religion of Life in Everyday Speech* (London: SCM, 1999); *The Meaning of It All in Everyday Speech* (London: SCM, 1999); and *Kingdom Come in Everyday Speech* (London: SCM, 2000).

8 Gerd Theissen, *The Sign Language of Faith,* p. 20.

9 For weekly examples of Christian responses to contemporary culture, see the Damaris Trust project at the website: www.damaris.org/cw/index.html.

## Chapter 14

1 Brother Aidan, 'The meaning and use of icons', in *Orthodox Outlook* (Vol. 40, No. 6, Issue 40, 1991), pp. 20–3.

2 I am grateful to Heather Boyd for the letter and for this observation.
3 John Davies, 'Meditation', in Neil Taylor and Joan Bloodworth (eds), *Living with Posters* (Ikon Productions and USPG, 1980), p. 20.
4 Thomas Troeger, *Imagining a Sermon* (Nashville: Abingdon, 1990), pp. 61–5. Used by permission.

## Chapter 15

1 Edward R. Tufte, 'The cognitive style of PowerPoint' (Cheshire, CT: Graphics Press).
2 Projecting visuals raises questions of copyright. I recommend contact with two organizations: Christian Copyright Licensing International and Christian Video Licensing International – www.ccli.co.uk and info@ccli.co.uk.
3 Jamie Byrom, in a private communication.
4 Ian Parker, 'Absolute Powerpoint: Can a software package edit our thoughts?', in *The New Yorker*, 28 May 2001.

## Chapter 16

1 Robert Pagliari, *Fourteen Steps to Dynamic Preaching* (Liguori: Liguori Publishing, 1993), p. 55.
2 Robert Pagliari, *Fourteen Steps to Dynamic Preaching*, p. 57.
3 Dave McClellan, 'Say It With Flowers . . . and IV Bags', *Christianity Today International/Leadership Journal* (Winter 2002, Vol. 24, No. 1), p. 53.
4 From a sermon by Andrew Trigger.
5 Catherine Fox, *Angels and Men* (London: Hamish Hamilton, 1995), p. 28.
6 I am grateful to my former colleague, Steve Croft, for the outline of this address.
7 This is an eyewitness account from Revd Dale Hanson.
8 See Sharon J. Swain, *The Sermon Slot Year 1* and *The Sermon Slot Year 2* (London: SPCK, 1992, 1993), especially *Year 1*, pp. 10–11.

## Chapter 17

1 James R. Nieman, 'Preaching that drives people from the church', *Currents in Theology and Mission* (No. 20, 1993), pp. 106–15.
2 Robert Pagliari, *Fourteen Steps to Dynamic Preaching* (Liguori: Liguori Publications, 1993), p. 62.
3 Evans E. Crawford, *The Hum: Call and Response in African American Preaching* (Nashville: Abingdon Press, 1995), pp. 37–8.
4 Laurence A. Wagley, *Preaching with the Small Congregation* (Nashville: Abingdon Press, 1989), p. 10.
5 Jeremy Thomson, *Preaching as Dialogue: Is the Sermon a Sacred Cow?*, Grove Pastoral Series 68 (Grove Books, 1996).
6 Tim Stratford, *Interactive Preaching, Opening the Word then Listening*, Grove Worship Series 144 (Grove Books, 1998).
7 Brian Pearson, 'Interactive methods of preaching', in Geoffrey Hunter, Gethin Thomas and Stephen Wright (eds), *A Preacher's Companion* (Oxford: The Bible Reading Fellowship, 2004), pp. 107–10.

**Chapter 18**

1 John Leach, *Responding to Preaching,* Grove Worship Series 139 (Grove Books, 1997, 2001), pp. 10–13.

2 Walter Brueggemann (ed. Patrick Miller), *The Psalms and the Life of Faith* (Minneapolis: Fortress Press, 1995), p. 118.

3 Henry Mitchell, *Celebration and Experience in Preaching* (Nashville: Abingdon Press, 1990), p. 12.

4 Henry Mitchell, *Celebration and Experience in Preaching,* p. 68.

5 I am grateful for many of these ideas to Tim Sanderson, Youth and Children's Worker at St Nicholas' Church, Durham.

6 From a sermon by Andrew Trigger.

7 For ideas about using embodying action in prayerful response, see two books by John Pritchard: *The Intercessions Handbook* (London: SPCK, 1997) and *The Second Intercessions Handbook* (London: SPCK, 2004).

8 Reported in the *Church of England Newspaper.*

9 The Emmaus Project has produced a number of books which help congregations to work collaboratively on biblical material, drawing together sermon, worship, individual reading and group discussion. See, for example, Steve Croft, *The Lord is Risen!* and David Day, *Christ Our Life: The Letter to the Colossians,* both published by National Society/Church House Publishing.

10 Laurence A. Wagley, *Preaching with the Small Congregation* (Nashville: Abingdon Press, 1989), p. 99.

11 Laurence A. Wagley, *Preaching with the Small Congregation,* p. 64.

12 Catherine Byrom, *The Pastoral Care of Those Who Are Losing Faith,* unpublished MA dissertation, Nottingham University, May 2004.

13 Chrysostom, *Homilies on the Gospel of John,* 3.